THE FOOTPRINTS
OF
ELEPHANT BILL

THE FOOTPRINTS

OF

ELEPHANT BILL

BY

SUSAN WILLIAMS

WILLIAM KIMBER
46 WILTON PLACE, LONDON, S.W.1

First published in 1962 by
WILLIAM KIMBER AND CO. LIMITED
46 Wilton Place, London, S.W.1

MADE AND PRINTED IN GREAT BRITAIN BY PURNELL AND SONS, LTD.
PAULTON (SOMERSET) AND LONDON

AUTHOR'S NOTE

I would not like to let this book appear without thanking Mrs. William Kimber for the indispensable help she gave me in reviving and recording my memories of the past.

CONTENTS

		Page
I.	The Uncle from Burma	11
II.	Prelude in Rangoon	18
III.	Uncle Pop's Tiger	24
IV.	The Buffalo Killer	31
V.	The Shadow of a Scourge	37
VI.	Meeting in the Jungle	44
VII.	Happy Voyage	53
VIII.	A New Life with Jim	59
IX.	A Household on the Trek	69
X.	Soapsuds and Elephant Surgery	76
XI.	The Heart of the Forests	81
XII.	Elephants at Work	90
XIII.	The Jungle Strikes	99
XIV.	The Rule of the *Nats*	104
XV.	The Doc	111
XVI.	A Predicament with Poison	117
XVII.	The Dancing Thakin	123
XVIII.	Through the Teak Forests	129
XIX.	The Python in the Pool	134
XX.	When Sorrows Come	141
XXI.	The Little Jungle Wallah	147
XXII.	The Tuskers Save the Bridge	152
XXIII.	The Most Intelligent Animal	165

CONTENTS

		Page
XXIV.	War Comes to the East	172
XXV.	The Exodus Begins	179
XXVI.	Refugee Cavalcade	186
XXVII.	Relentless March	192
XXVIII.	Elephant Leader	199
XXIX.	Elephants at War	207
XXX.	A Life to the Full	214

ILLUSTRATIONS

Elephant Bill . . . . . *Facing page* 48
　　　By courtesy of Greville Howard

Uncle Pop 49

Jim's leading travelling elephants coming into camp . 49

Baby elephant doing its first travelling job . . 64

Young elephant in training crush 65

Still a bit uncertain of the 'hmit' position . . . 65

The young oozie with his baby elephant . . . 96

Climbing up a ridge to reach a log . . . 96

Travelling elephant being unloaded . . . 97

What a height to climb for a tit-bit! . . . 112

Baby elephant seeking shade under its mother . . 113

Bath time 113

In the cool of the evening—the day's work done . 144

Unloading stores beside the Chindwin . . . 144

They push 145

And they pull 145

"I was in it up to my ears" 160

In the logging camp 161

Treating a crushed toenail 161

"What mother does I can do too" 176

A downy baby has finished its bath 176

9

Laying the foundations for a bridge in wartime   .   177

The rains have come   177

A pile of logs that only elephants could disentangle   .   192

Jim with Susan, a fortnight before his death   .   .   193

Treve on a jungle trek, with San Pyu in foreground   .   193

Chapter I

THE UNCLE FROM BURMA

M Y HUSBAND often used to say to me that for a man to be really happy and fulfilled he must have one outstanding and special interest in life—"And it might as well be elephants as anything else," he would add, because that happened to be his.

In fact, his interests were unusually varied and numerous and the fact that elephants took first place probably only came about by chance. He had always been devoted to all animals, but it was his work in the Burma teak forests that brought him into direct contact with these particular ones. He certainly grew to understand them perhaps more than anyone else alive at the time, and in the Second World War, after the Japs had invaded Burma, he was called upon by the Fourteenth Army under General Slim to be Elephant Adviser.

Whereas sappers might take over a week to build a bridge across one of the hundreds of small rivers that traverse this country, his elephants could do the same job in a matter of twenty-four hours and were indispensable in all sorts of ways. He became known throughout the army as Elephant Bill— a name that clung to him for the rest of his life.

As for me—if I had been told early on in life that I was to meet the man I was to marry in a remote part of the Burma jungle and that elephants were going to be one of my consuming interests I should hardly have believed it.

The whole thing was, I suppose, put in motion one day about two years before when I was in my early twenties and living a quiet, uneventful English country life.

I remember it well. It was late October and the french windows were wide open. Only the garden showed signs of approaching winter with its bedraggled clumps of Michaelmas daisies and dahlias. It was 'a day lent', as they say in Cornwall, and, as I was to find to my joy, a day of promise in more ways than one.

I was spending a fortnight's holiday at home with my grandmother at Evesham. She had announced at breakfast-time that a nephew of hers, Stephen Hopwood, home on leave from Burma, was coming to tea that afternoon and would I be sure to be there, as she would like me to meet him. He was always known in the family as Uncle Pop, and I had only met him once before when I was a schoolgirl.

Four-thirty, and tea was all laid: the lovely red and white Royal Worcester teacups, which I still drink my tea out of to-day, were all in readiness on the glistening brass-topped Benares tea table, with the usual fresh scones and home-made cake.

I don't think Uncle Pop noticed any of it. He arrived punctually and when greetings were over came quickly to the reason for his visit. He was due to return to Burma in May and the niece who had been with him before was about to get married. He wanted another one to take her place, and to go with him on the jungle tours which were a part of his job.

He turned to me. "Would you like to come?" he asked.

I didn't have time to reply. He took it for granted I would accept.

My grandmother was thrilled. She had herself been in India in the old sailing-ship days and had had such a wonderful time out there that she thought it must be every young girl's dream.

"How wonderful for you, Sue," she said. "You will love it."

Granny was a wonderful person—warm, loving and giving. She had come to keep house for my father, who was her eldest son, when my mother had died in the 1918 flu epidemic. She left all her friends and a life of ease to look after us six children, the youngest seven and the eldest fourteen; but we all loved her dearly and were so proud of her, she had such dignity. She always wore ankle-length voluminous skirts and in an under-petticoat was a large pocket where she kept her purse. One of my most vivid memories of her is the way she used to pick up her dress to find it.

She was my 'mother' for seventeen years, and all she wanted was our happiness.

I wasn't absolutely sure in my own mind about Uncle Pop's invitation, but the family's enthusiasm carried the day and it was decided I should go. Only gradually did it dawn on me what an adventure this might be.

My uncle fired a series of questions at me. Horses were his be-all and end-all in life, so the first question was—could I ride? Then, did I know anything of the East, etc., etc.?

To them all the answer was No; but undeterred he went on planning. It was arranged that first of all I was to join him in London where he would arrange riding lessons for me and help me over buying my kit.

Uncle Pop got up to go. Coming back into the room after seeing him off, it was as if something vital had left us all. Everything seemed so ordinary and flat again. Although only of medium height, he was a man of commanding personality. His clear skin and quizzically keen eye advertised his fitness, and at fifty he had the look of a much younger man. His hair was still black and thick, except for some wisps of grey at the temples, his movements brisk, his attitude always determined, and at times dogmatic.

That evening I bombarded my grandmother with questions, chiefly about my uncle. She told me he had gone into the Indian Forest Service as a young man and had spent all his time since in Burma, except during the First World War, when he had joined the army. His wife Helen had been out in the East with him until 1920, when she died suddenly

All who knew him said that he had altered tremendously after her death, becoming very shut away and reserved. In fact in later years no one ever realised he had been married as he never mentioned her name.

He had done well in the Burma Forest Service and was now due to go back to a new appointment as Chief Conservator. This meant, among other things, that he would tour wherever he liked, as all jungle forest areas in the country were his responsibility.

At this time, except for a visit to a married sister who lived in Jersey, I had never been out of England. I was now going away for at least two and a half years—that is, if I stayed on until Uncle Pop was due for his next leave—but I had no qualms about leaving home for so long. There was only one worry in the back of my mind—my grandmother was old, nearly eighty, but wonderfully fit, and I did want her to be there when I came home again.

Meanwhile I had to give up my job. I had been trained as a children's nurse, and was now looking after two small girls. I enjoyed this, but it was not really the sort of work I wanted to do as I much preferred an outdoor life.

I was in such a state of suppressed excitement that it was hard going back again and settling down to normal routine. However, my employers could not have been more helpful and it was agreed that I should be allowed to leave at the end of the month to give me time to prepare for the trip.

On my way home a few doubts settled in. Was I mad to be setting off for a country and a life I knew nothing about, with an uncle who was virtually a complete stranger and whom I did not take to overmuch, anyway? I wondered how it would all work out.

*　　*　　*

I was to find out a little of what life would be like with him during that first trip to London.

His energy was unbounded, considering he never had any

14

regular meals except breakfast; at this meal he always ate great spoonfuls of *Bemax*, and perhaps it was this which gave him his tremendous vigour. He took me walking for miles on the London pavements, and only when I was ready to drop and ravenously hungry did I have the courage to tell him so.

I don't think half the time he even realised I was there beside him. He would tell me story after story, all of which I was to hear repeated over and over again during the time I was with him.

He did, however, take the greatest interest in my riding kit, coming with me when I was measured for it and insisting that I had the very best—I was to look the part, anyway.

In spite of this distant, autocratic manner, there was something that appealed to me about Uncle Pop. Though outwardly self-sufficient, I could feel a certain loneliness about him and a need for company—but I rather wondered if I would be adequate to fill this need.

*   *   *

A large handful of periodicals was thrust onto my lap as our train steamed out of Victoria Station three months later. I scarcely looked at them, there was so much else to see.

It was a lovely April morning and the countryside looked washed and fresh in its new spring green, and the warm sun streamed through the carriage window; a memory stored for stifling hot days later on, when just to close one's eyes was to conjure up the freshness and beauty of it all. The banks were studded with primroses and bluebells, just showing colour. It was joyous, it was England, it was springtime.

We were on the first lap of the journey to Marseilles, where we were to join our ship. Uncle Pop always travelled by P. & O. Line, as all the stewards were Goanese and once aboard he felt he was back in the East again, where he could command and be obeyed.

I saw little of him on the voyage: the only date I had to keep with him was our morning march three and a half times round the deck for daily exercise. The usual shipboard life was new to me and kept me happily amused for the two weeks we were on the boat.

I was quite sorry when we reached Bombay and had to board the famous Blue Train for our two-day journey across the dusty plains of India. It was a completely strange world to me, and even the small things like movable cane chairs instead of the usual carriage seats struck me as being odd and exciting.

How hot it was, and the countryside did nothing to make one feel cooler—red dusty fields for mile after mile, and at each halt the platforms littered with travellers—sleeping shrouded forms looking rather like overgrown chrysalises. The hardness of the stone seemed to make little difference to the soundness of their rest. Miserable native dogs in all stages of mange and emaciation were scrounging round for scraps amongst them, and only the creamy humped cattle seemed well fed. These, being sacred, were left to wander where they willed, even on the railway.

When I lowered the window we were besieged by beggars—one-eyed, one-armed, one-legged—they were there in their legions. I was horrified by this impoverished throng of humanity, but when I dropped small coins into their begging-bowls it brought even more of them swarming round.

My concern only caused Uncle Pop amusement, and he told me to close the window.

"You will have to get used to this sort of thing," he said.

It was all so commonplace to him—just part of the pattern of things he had long ceased to notice—but to me it seemed poignant human tragedy.

Arriving in Calcutta, our train journey over, we now had to board the little steamer which crossed the Bay of Bengal to Rangoon. So far I had enjoyed the journey immensely; and as neither the sea voyage nor the heat on the long train journey had any ill effect on me at all, I fancied myself a seasoned traveller. But I certainly had it coming to me, for the little boat we were now on ran into the tail end of a cyclone about halfway across the bay, and it was as though all hell had broken loose.

I would never have thought it possible that any small boat could have been battered about by such a tornado and still hold together; I was very ill, and ashamed of being so frightened. My only comfort was to find out later on from Uncle Pop that even he had succumbed. I must say that as we eventually steamed into the calm waters at the mouth of the Rangoon River, I noticed that he had lost a lot of his jauntiness and did not look quite his usual spruce self.

The little ship ploughed on for several hours through the murky brown waters of the estuary before the banks of the river came into view and in the distant haze the lush green land of Burma slowly emerged.

Long before we reached Rangoon I caught my first glimpse of the beautiful golden dome of the Shwe Dagon Pagoda rising high above the city. This monumental shrine to Buddha is the first thing one sees in the distance, and is covered in pure gold from base to summit and studded with jewels.

Glistening in the brilliant sunlight, it looked magnificent. I knew it was the glowing heart of Burma, and was thrilled.

Chapter II

PRELUDE IN RANGOON

ON UP the river we steamed and soon the peaceful green paddy fields on either side began to give way to various mills and industrial buildings and the huge oil storage tanks and refineries belonging to the Burma oil companies. We passed by the saw-mills belonging to the teak firms working in the country, and we were near enough to see the logs being eased out of the water by huge elephants—magnificent beasts, their tusks banded with metal for protection.

Uncle Pop, seeing how interested I was, explained to me how these logs had been floated down from the jungle, sometimes taking years on the way. First of all, the trees in the forests were ringed or girdled at the base; teak wood has to be dead before it will float, and this prevented the sap flowing up into them, and killed them.

There was then a wait of three years before they were felled and elephants were able to drag them to the nearest stream to wait till the rains came to float them away to join the main rivers. Here they were made into rafts and eventually found their way down to these timber mills in Rangoon.

As we approached the port the river became densely populated with craft of all shapes and sizes: little coastal trading steamers, big ocean-going liners, sailing dhows, catamarans, and the ubiquitous sampan. These precarious little craft seemed to wend their way in and out of the other shipping at a phenomenal speed. They were propelled by one oar at the stern and were decorated with painted eyes at the bows which, I was told, were to help the helmsman in the dark.

At the dockside, we were met by Uncle Pop's car, which drove us through the modern wide thoroughfares of Rangoon city. Not quite the narrow, mysterious Eastern streets I had imagined. But the colour and noise were all there, and the brilliant silks that both men and women were wearing were startling in the tropical sunshine.

The whole place was a bustle of humanity; Chinese, Indians and Burmans were all jostling each other on the pavements. The heat was terrific—one felt as though one had gone into a hot greenhouse and shut the door behind one. I was surprised to notice—and this always struck me all the years I was in Burma—how, in spite of the heat, the neat little Burmese women had a wonderful knack of always looking cool and soignée.

The traffic was thick, an amazing mixture of smart cars, rickshaws and hand-propelled carts, and amongst them all the slow-moving bullock carts plodded along unperturbed. I was amused to see that the buses, which were crammed with passengers, had animals such as tigers and snakes painted on the front, showing the various localities they served, instead of the usual route numbers or place names.

Uncle Pop's pleasant verandahed house stood in a residential avenue about five miles the other side of the city. On arrival, I was immediately shown up to my bedroom. It was sparsely furnished, with just the bare necessities—a black iron bed draped with a mosquito net stood in the middle of the red-tiled floor. It was as bleak as a convent cell. The only ornamental thing in the room was a young Burmese girl, who came forward to meet me, smiling a greeting.

Uncle Pop turned to me, saying, "What do you think of it all, Miss Poppy?" This was what he called all the nieces who had stayed out here with him—it saved having to remember our individual names.

I thought the room was rather like a scullery, but this did not worry me so much as this Burmese ayah, and what I was supposed to do with her. I was not used to being waited on and I

gathered that she could speak no English, and as yet I knew
only very few words of Burmese.

"Need I have her?" I asked Uncle Pop.

"Of course you must," he said.

I was soon to realise what a joy it was to have her around;
she was so quiet and self-effacing and knew instinctively how to
help me without being told. She looked rather like a pretty little
doll, in her gay silk shirt and spotless muslin coat with dangling
glass buttons. Her name was Ma Shwe, and we soon became
firm friends.

We had arrived in Rangoon in the middle of May, the season
of the mango showers; the atmosphere felt like a turkish bath,
sticky and humid. Insect life abounded, and in the evening
especially they were attracted by the bright lights and com-
mitted suicide in their millions.

Dinner that first night was a nightmare. Insects fell in the
soup, crawled on the fish, and ran down the back of my neck.
Uncle Pop laughed when, in desperation, I said I must go to
bed. I was thankful when the mosquito net was finally lowered
and I felt safe at last.

Having lived a bachelor existence for so long, Uncle Pop had
grown set in his way of life and hated any form of change;
but I soon began to get used to his ways and to know what was
expected of me.

As long as I was up in the morning to ride with him, and
home by tea-time when he returned from his office, he minded
little what I did between times. He would send me off by
myself to parties at the houses of people I had never met before;
being shy, I hated this at first, and only went because Uncle
Pop more or less ordered me to do so. However, girls were in
great demand out here and before long I got to know quite a lot
of people and began to love the life.

Uncle Pop liked my company as long as I sat and listened,
but he didn't expect me to express any views; his two great
interests were forestry and horses, and every day immediately
tea was finished, he would go down to the stables. He had had

these built at the end of the garden and was always getting complaints from the residents nearby because of the flies they attracted.

The rest of the garden was entirely given over to growing titbits for these horses. Their hay and oats were specially shipped out from England, just as Uncle Pop's food was—he did not like oriental dishes.

He kept six beautiful English horses and he never tired of talking of them. His favourite was a great black gelding called Stealaway; he was a fearless rider, and mounted on this animal he felt and looked as if he could defy the world.

One morning, about a week after we had arrived in Rangoon, I got up as usual at six-thirty and, in the warmth of the morning, I wandered out onto the verandah and was surprised to see that the ground outside looked quite white, almost as if there had been a hoar frost.

Uncle Pop explained that the whiteness was caused by millions of ants' wings. During the evening the first early showers of the coming monsoon had penetrated the hard red ground, and the flying ants had pushed their way through the softened soil. They were unable to mate except in flight, and once this had been achieved, they shed their wings like leaves off a tree in autumn. From then onwards they became crawling grub-like creatures; on the ground again, the nuptial flight having lasted only a few hours, their gossamer finery was gone for ever.

That evening was to be Uncle Pop's first dinner party since his return and I asked him if he would like me to work out a menu with the cook.

"No need for that," he said. "I always have the same thing—it saves a lot of bother—but you can arrange the daffodils if you like."

"What daffodils?" I asked.

"Oh, they are somewhere in my boxes outside," he said. "Go and ask San Baw."

With this he buried his head back in his paper again, which

I had come to know well as a sign that he had finished with me for the moment.

I went out and asked San Baw whatever Uncle Pop had meant. He knew at once.

"It's the paper daffodils, Thakinma," he said. "Master never likes to give a dinner party without them in the middle of the table."

He went out and brought back a rather squashed cardboard box. The paper daffodils were truly dreadful—crumpled and dusty, with most of the colour faded out of them. I thought to myself: how pathetic a bachelor can be, and decided to go out and buy him some fresh roses.

"Throw these awful bits of paper away," I said to San Baw, handing him back the box. "I hate artificial flowers anyway, and if Thakin has a liking for them, I will buy him some that are a bit more presentable than these."

On his return from the office, Uncle Pop went into the dining-room to inspect the dinner table. I had taken a good deal of trouble in arranging some exquisite pink rosebuds which I had managed to find in the bazaar. He took one look at them, and turned on me furiously.

"What are those doing in the middle of the table?" he said. Before I had time to explain, he shouted for San Baw.

"Where are my daffodils?"

I shook in my shoes because I could see he was really angry, and I could have kissed San Baw when he came back with them in his hands.

"Throw those things away," said Uncle Pop, pointing at the roses, "and put my flowers back where they should be." And with that, he brushed past me out of the room.

I was completely baffled. It wasn't until much later that I realised what all the fuss had been about. We were halfway through dinner; everyone had been patiently listening to story after story and Uncle Pop was telling yet another one.

Ending dramatically, he stood up and held out his hand towards the bowl in the middle of the table, intoning "Daffodils, that come before the swallow dares, and take the winds of March with beauty . . ." It illustrated his point perfectly, and he sat down triumphant.

He turned his head towards me and gave me a steely stare as much as to say: You nearly robbed me of my success. I am afraid at this point it was too much for me, and I could not prevent myself from smiling.

Uncle Pop's face changed to a look of puzzled surprise at my reaction, but somehow or other he managed to smile back.

From then onwards I saw to it that the dejected paper daffodils took pride of place at every dinner party.

CHAPTER III

UNCLE POP'S TIGER

BEFORE I left England I had visualised life out here with Uncle Pop as being one long jungle tour: dense forests, full of wild animals, and snakes curled round the branches of almost every tree, just as I had seen in films as a child.

He hadn't bothered to tell me anything about life in Rangoon, or even that we should be spending some little time there before setting out on our first expedition. However, I was now completely immersed in a life of party-going, and perhaps Uncle Pop thought things were becoming a bit too hectic. He suddenly came back from his office one evening and announced casually that in two days' time we were setting off.

I quickly had to cancel all the dates I had made, and had to rush round the shops getting all that was needed. I had not brought the proper jungle clothes with me, as Uncle Pop had assured me he could provide me with the right things when the time came. Not knowing him quite so well then, I had thought no more about it.

Now, as I stood and looked at myself in the glass, dressed in the extraordinary things he had found for me to wear, I was horrified. I looked exactly like someone out of the Stanley-Livingstone era. Khaki plus fours, khaki shirts buttoned to the wrists, thick puttees and canvas boots, and on top a large double-brimmed felt hat.

However, Uncle Pop couldn't have cared less how I looked, and only remarked, "How wonderfully protected from all pests you will be, Miss Poppy."

24

I only hoped nobody I knew would ever see me in this crazy get-up. To top it all, he provided me with a large bamboo matting basket to carry all my belongings.

A day and night had to be spent in the train to reach the remote wayside halt in the jungle from where our tour was to start. We took several servants with us, including Ma Shwe, my little ayah, and a cook.

I was very impressed on arrival to find jungle ponies and bullock carts to carry our kit, all ready and waiting for us. It brought home to me that in his work Uncle Pop, being Chief Conservator, was quite an important person.

I had seen many bullock carts in Rangoon, but I had never realised before what a noise they made with their solid creaking unoiled wheels. Uncle told me these wheels were purposely never greased and that each pair had its own individual sound. Thus, when nearing his village, a cartman's wife was warned of his approach. Sometimes the wheels weren't even round, but the drivers seemed unperturbed by the bumps of the rutted track.

Riding our ponies, we left the sunlight of the open railway line for the cloistered gloom of the forest, and rode along a path through dense bamboo clumps, their feather tops intermingling to form a tunnel. Above these grew massive trees shutting out the sunlight. Underneath it was cool green and rather eerie, and only occasionally did we see glimpses of brilliant blue to show there was still a sunlit sky above. The ponies' hooves stirred the dry leaves underfoot as they climbed up one steep hillside and down the next.

The Burma jungle is a thickly timbered mass of parallel ridges and valleys; as we climbed to one of the higher of these ridges and looked over the vast stretches of forest, it was as though the whole world was nothing but trees. A vast continent of green for miles and miles in every direction—it was breath-takingly beautiful now, in the early morning, when the mists still lay wreathed in the valleys below.

One knew the whole thing was teeming with wild life—tiger, bear, leopard, bison, deer, monkeys and snakes. I had expected the forest to be alive with their cries and those of the birds, and it was one of the things that surprised me most that first day and for the whole of my time in the jungle, how much, despite their presence, they eluded human eyes and ears.

The silence is more awe-inspiring than any sound. It is as though thousands of eyes are watching unseen and not until darkness begins to fall and an eerie light covers the whole scene is the silence broken by the shrilling of myriads of cicadas—a sort of thick-bellied insect—who keep up their ceaseless chant until darkness falls.

As we came into a valley again and were crossing a dried-up stream bed, Uncle Pop got off his pony, saying, "Come and have a look at these."

Under the high overhanging banks, where the dew had fallen heavily, he showed me some pug marks in the still damp sand.

"These were made by a tiger," he said. "It must have passed this way in the last few hours; they are quite fresh."

I asked him how he knew this. He walked up the river bed a few yards, and then pointed to some other large hoof marks.

"These are the slot marks of a sambhur deer," he said, "and you can tell they were made some little time ago by the cob-webs that have been spun right across them.

"The tiger, having prowled around all night hunting for prey, probably came down to this stream in the early hours of the morning, feeling thirsty. Finding it dry, he would have wandered off up the ravine to look for some place where there was still a trickle of water."

Uncle Pop looked at me with his dry, quizzical, half-amused expression and said, "Frightened, Miss Poppy? No need to worry, a tiger hardly ever attacks man in the day-time. They have more reason to be frightened of us than we of them. It's only very rarely that an old or wounded animal, who is un-able to travel as fast as he used to, may get desperate with hunger and go to lie up near a village in order to catch any-thing that may come his way. He's sure to be an ex-cattle killer who has got used to seeing herdsmen, and so has lost his inborn dread of human beings. But he has wonderful discrimination, and if a man is armed he'll run for miles. Even when hunted, though, the tiger will show a sudden audacity—I've seen one grab hold of a bullock while itself being very hotly chased."

Uncle Pop then sank back into his usual silence—but his keen bright eyes were ever on the watch for bison or deer or other big game. The only thing we saw for the rest of the ride were a herd of saing, the wild cattle of Burma. We were quite close to them, having taken them by surprise as we came over a rise in the path, and had a wonderful view of them as, with a terrific noise and stampeding, they flashed away through the trees.

Five miles on, we came to a sudden fenced clearing in very dense jungle, in the middle of which stood an empty teak house raised from the ground on posts. This was a Forest Rest House in which we were to spend two nights. Many like it were to be found throughout the jungle, and although they were provided by the government forest department for the use of their personnel on tour, they were only sparsely furnished with teak cane-chairs and webbing beds. However, they were quite adequate for a few nights.

For some reason, the small lavatory hut was always built outside the boundary fence, about thirty yards from the Rest House; all right to visit during the day, but when it became dark I really hated going there, especially as Uncle Pop had casually mentioned to me to be sure to shine my torch around before entering. Pythons liked to choose the seat to curl up on, and the walls were favourite hiding places for scorpions and large evil-looking spiders. Needless to say, I visited it as infrequently as I possibly could.

Inside the fence I felt perfectly safe, and I thought that first night in the jungle was one of the most wonderful experiences I had ever had. Uncle Pop had taken the only two candles and was writing with one on either side of him, so I sat for hours in the dark, watching the moonlight turning the giant tree trunks all around into huge pillars of silver. I found it hard to drag myself away to bed, but eventually went to my room and lay with the doors wide open, listening to the jungle sounds.

Next morning I heard Uncle Pop calling me from the verandah.

"Have you slept with your doors open like that?" he said.

"Yes," I told him; "the moonlight was so wonderful that I could not shut it out."

"Come with me. I'll show you something that will make you keep your doors closed in future," he said.

He took me down the wide verandah steps, and there in the sandy ground were fresh leopard pug marks. The animal had prowled all round the Rest House in the night.

"Don't you realise," he said, "that the verandah is an easy leap for a leopard?"

We had no dog with us, which is what really interests a leopard, so presumably there was nothing worth jumping for. However, it was too near not to take precautions, and he made it plain that he thought I was a complete boob.

Next morning we set off again; Uncle Pop was inspecting a new forest area that was shortly to be worked by one of the teak firms. We hadn't gone far along the track when a loose pony, which was surprisingly far away from any habitation, trotted up behind us. It had probably strayed from a village and had been grazing near where we passed, and liked the idea of company.

I was ahead, and Uncle Pop shouted, "That damn animal will be a nuisance; shoo it away, Miss Poppy."

I thought it would return the way it had come, instead of which it cantered ahead. We did not think about it any more, and were astonished when, rounding a bend about a quarter of a mile on, we found the pony lying across the track dead, its head nearly severed from its body. It had been killed by a tiger which had already started to make a meal of it and had evidently been frightened away at our approach. It could only just have left, as the pony's nerves were still twitching and an eight-inch square of skin had been neatly removed from its rump.

"That's because," said Uncle Pop, "a tiger always begins to feed from the tail end."

The sight of it appalled me, especially as I felt we had shooed this poor pony right into the jaws of the tiger and to its horrible death. But Uncle Pop assured me that its jugular vein had been cut in two by one powerful blow of the tiger's forepaw and that death must have been instantaneous.

He himself was in a great state of excitement. "This may give me a wonderful chance to shoot that tiger," he said. "There is no time to build a platform up in a tree, as I would do in the ordinary way. I am sure that old cat will be back quite soon to finish his meal, so we'll have to hurry."

He shouted to one of the Burmans with us and told him that directly the bullock carts came along he must go and get two camp chairs from amongst our things and have them tied in the fork of the tree behind us. The pony's carcase was to be tied to another tree nearby, to prevent the tiger dragging it away.

Early that evening Uncle Pop and I both sat perched in the branches in absolute silence—waiting. It was twilight, and one could feel the jungle beginning to awake, led by the loud chorus of cicadas which kept up their constant shrilling through the still air.

A young squirrel came tripping across the bough of a tree opposite, and I turned to draw Uncle Pop's attention to it. He silenced me with a threatening look—I hardly dared to breathe.

It seemed ages before we heard a rustle and heavy footfalls. Then, in the fast fading light, the head of a tiger appeared. He stalked round the tree and seized on the dead pony. But before he could drag it away, he heard the sound of the rifle being lifted and looked up, startled. Uncle Pop fired—the tiger leapt into the air, then turned and bounded up the bank at the side of the track, where we could see it rolling over to lick its wound. Uncle Pop fired again, but it was out of range and sprang away into the undergrowth.

It was rare for Uncle Pop to miss a sitting shot like this, and he was angry and also worried, as this was a much-used track and a hungry, wounded animal was a real danger.

My immediate reaction was that we ought to go after it and finish it off, but he soon put me right about that and told me that a wounded tiger was not a thing to take chances with. Luckily we were near enough to the rest house for him to fire three shots into the air as a signal for one or two of the Burmans there to come and escort us back.

It was quite dark by now, and as they rushed excitedly forward by the light of their bamboo flares, expecting to see a dead tiger, they were thoroughly disappointed to find only the now stinking carcase of the pony.

Next day search parties were organised to go out and find the tiger. It took two days to run it to ground, and Uncle Pop shot it where it had gone to earth in a hole, and from which it eventually had to be dug out. He did not allow me to go on this expedition, and in a way I felt glad that I had not been there when he described to me how this magnificent tigress in the height of fitness had come to such an ignominious and undignified end. Needless to say, Uncle Pop only felt he had done a good service in ridding the jungle of just one more dangerous animal.

When we passed that way two days later, it shook me to see that all that was left of that fat shining little pony I had driven ahead of me along the path was a perfectly clean dry carcase-frame of bones. The vultures had picked it bare.

Chapter IV

THE BUFFALO KILLER

UNCLE POP's tour was to last about a month. I had already had some experience of his indefatigable walking habits—on the London pavements—and now, after three weeks in the jungle and in spite of the heat, he seemed to have more stamina than ever.

He was in his element; there was little he did not know about trees and forestry, and he was for ever on the watch for wild life, but he seemed wrapped up in his own thoughts, which he seldom passed on to me, and I always had the feeling that I must not disturb them—so, for a great part of the time, we walked or rode in silence.

He did not want to be bothered much with food either, and was quite happy to march all day with nothing more than a couple of pieces of *Ryvita* and a cup of tea, and expected me to do the same. None of this worried me, as the whole thing was so new and full of interest, and by now I had grown to understand his whims and ways.

We were seeing the jungle during the winter season when the sun shone for three successive months and the days were like a perfect, if hot, English summer. Most of the streams and small rivers were nearly dry but we found welcome shade as we climbed up the wadis deep in shadow. Their precipitous sides were hung with feathery maidenhair fern from top to bottom. Moss and lichen clung to every rock and crevice, and one had the feeling one was walking through a refreshing cool green tunnel. The only sound was water, as it trickled and splashed into the gorge beyond, where there was only the silence of the large dark pools.

One day we were coming towards the mouth of such a gorge when Uncle Pop stopped dead and pointed with his stick. A group of wild elephants were idling on the sandy river bed below—they evidently had not caught wind of us. These were the first wild elephants I had seen and they looked serene and contented as they stood and enjoyed the cool shallow water.

This is the season when fodder is plentiful for all wild game and the water in the streams is crystal clear. I had seldom seen such a peaceful scene, and was surprised when Uncle Pop turned to me and whispered in my ear, "If they should turn and charge, go and stand at once behind the largest tree you can get to, and stay stock still. Elephants close their eyes when they charge, and having gone past they are not likely to turn back on their tracks again, but will be glad to get away."

I could hardly believe there was any danger. However, the bull elephant, obviously the leader of the herd, must suddenly have scented us as he started banging his trunk on the ground by way of warning—it made an astonishing hollow ringing sound, like a hammer on an anvil.

The herd at once took up a rigid listening attitude, their great ears spread out like gigantic fans. We remained absolutely still, and after some seconds they decided that the danger was past and started to pick up sand and blow it over themselves. They then turned round one after the other, and went slowly lumbering off in the opposite direction.

"We were lucky to have seen that herd," said Uncle Pop, "and lucky too that they did not hear us. One seldom gets a chance to see wild elephants, and in any case they are not the sort of characters one would choose to have an encounter with."

I thought to myself that this perhaps was one of the occasions when his perennial silence had paid off.

One day soon after, we had set up camp, this time in tents near a village. Uncle Pop had sent for the headman, as he wanted to speak to him about the illicit felling of teak. But the poor man had a big trouble of his own, and as soon as he arrived appealed for help.

The villagers were all in a great state of fear because of a tiger at large which had been marauding the village and killing their buffaloes. He told us that one of their best animals had been killed only the night before, and that they felt sure the tiger would return to its kill. This was great news for Uncle Pop. He was as pleased as punch; and went off right away to make arrangements for a platform to be built above the now stinking buffalo. His only worry was that the carcase had got a bit too high even for the tiger—who would prefer its meat freshly killed.

By evening everything was ready and once more we were perched aloft—this time slightly more comfortably, as at least there was room to turn round. Unfortunately though, we were situated downwind from the kill, and the sickly stench was overpowering and seemed to penetrate everywhere. We had taken sandwiches and a hot drink with us, but all appetite completely vanished, and I felt I would never smell sweet again.

We sat in absolute silence for hours, with no sign of any tiger. Uncle Pop eventually got tired of waiting and said we would take it in turns to have forty winks. He handed me the rifle and said, "Your watch first, Miss Poppy." He made himself as comfortable as possible in the confined space, and within minutes he was fast asleep and snoring.

I was terrified—it was brilliant moonlight and every leaf and creeper seemed alive. Also, the height of the machan platform from the ground seemed considerably less than it had done in the early evening. It flashed through my mind how Uncle Pop had told me that a six to eight foot leap for a leopard was nothing, and that they could even climb trees. The mosquitoes, too, were a menace; although I had smothered myself with citronella oil, as a counter-scent as much as a preventative, it did no good. They attacked face and hands mercilessly—it was almost impossible to keep still.

Suddenly the jungle was in tumult—a tiger roaring and a buffalo moaning in pain—the tiger had returned, but not to our kill. It had evidently found another stray animal, and I could hear it all happening but could see nothing. The noise woke Uncle Pop, and there was no more sleep for either of us after that. We could hear the tiger snarling ferociously as it devoured its prey, and could also hear occasionally a pathetic weak moan from the powerless victim. They were both just out of view, so there was no hope of a shot and we were imprisoned in our machan.

It was not until dawn came that there was a sudden silence; the tiger had gone with the coming of the morning light and we were eventually able to climb down. I was hardly able to move, my hands and legs were so swollen with insect bites.

The sight of the second buffalo still half alive was almost too much for me. The tiger had been unable to deal it a knock-out blow because of the thickness of its neck, and it lay feebly twitching its ears in a vain attempt to keep away the hordes of flies. Its tail was lying on the ground, dismembered from its body, and pounds of flesh had been eaten away from its rump —the tiger had indeed had fresh meat.

I turned to Uncle Pop. "For heaven's sake put it out of its misery as quickly as possible," I pleaded.

He did this at once, but he was already working out in his mind about having another machan built for the coming evening over this new kill. I found I couldn't take the slightest interest in his plans, and was appalled at the thought of going through the same thing all over again. I had had quite enough and was worn out.

Uncle was in fine fettle all day, and was convinced more than ever now that this tiger must be put an end to. He said, "One cannot let tiredness or anything of the sort stand in the way. This village will not have a moment's peace until it is dead."

I saw his point, and that evening found me back at his side, once again perched on the machan waiting for the tiger.

At three o'clock in the morning, after we had been there about ten hours, even he was tired and much to my relief said, "We are out of luck, Miss Poppy—come on, we won't wait any longer."

We climbed down, and by the light of a small hand-torch started on our way back through the jungle.

I shall always remember that three miles. I had never been out walking through the jungle at this hour before. The moonlight cast queer moving shadows through the undergrowth and there seemed rustling movements all around. I had even to admit to Uncle Pop that I was frightened, and anxious lest the same thing might happen to us that had happened to the wretched buffalo the night before.

I was rather surprised at his reply: "I expect you are scared, and so am I—but you can't spend time in the jungle and never expect to feel fear."

We had made arrangements to have our bedding rolls left that night in an uninhabited timber hut near the railway line which passed along near one side of the village; it was too far to get back to our camp. I had an awful feeling we might not be able to find the hut in the dark, but Uncle Pop was confident, and I was very relieved when we eventually came upon it. Immediately we entered the door I saw my bedding roll in the dim light laid out on a shelf formed by three planks near the door, and lay down thankfully. It might have been the best interior sprung mattress; I was asleep as soon as I laid down my head.

In the morning I was woken early by the sound of heavy snoring. My uncle was a great snorer, but this was even worse than usual. I sat up and looked round the corner of the upright beam—it was a horrid shock to see a black shiny head of hair quite unlike Uncle Pop's. I got out of bed and went over to have a nearer look. There, blissfully asleep in the corner, rolled in a blanket, was a Chinaman. Uncle Pop was nowhere to be seen. I dashed outside the hut, and there he was, convulsed with laughter. A fellow traveller in the jungle had bedded down for the night, unbeknown to us.

For some reason this episode tickled him tremendously. For the whole of the following day he kept repeating, "What an experience for you, Miss Poppy, what an experience! You must write home and tell the family about that—didn't you have a shock?"

It never occurred to him that this was a very tame experience for me compared with the tiger-shoot and the gruesome death of the buffalo, or the hair-raising walk through the jungle the night before.

Chapter V

THE SHADOW OF A SCOURGE

WE WERE walking near the village next day on our way back to camp when the headman came out to meet us. "I am sorry about that tiger," said Uncle Pop. "We tried our best, but I can't stay here any longer unfortunately—we have got to move on today as we are heading back towards home."

While they were talking an adorable little tawny red puppy came running towards us—it was one of the ugliest and most attractive little dogs I had ever seen. It immediately started to chew my bootlaces, and I fell for it in a big way. I picked it up and nuzzled its funny little head in my neck.

"I'd like to take him back with us," I said. "I wonder who he belongs to?"

"He doesn't belong to anyone in particular," said the headman. "Just one of our village dogs—take it with you if you want to."

"For goodness' sake, Miss Poppy, you don't want that— it's only a pariah dog," said Uncle Pop. "They look lovely as puppies, but they all become scraggy and hideous when they grow older. There's the danger of rabies, too—these native dogs are very susceptible to it."

But, since I had left home, I had missed having a dog of my own almost more than anything, and I begged him to give the headman a rupee and let me take it away. Rather grudgingly, he gave way.

That evening, back in camp, Uncle Pop started up again about the puppy.

"I know it's a dear little thing and you probably think I am fussing over nothing," he said, "but I don't think you know anything about rabies, do you?"

I had to admit that I really knew very little, just a vague idea that people went mad if they got it.

"Well, to anyone who has lived out East as long as I have," he said, "it is one of the few really haunting fears, especially if you have known people, as I have, who, having been bitten by these dogs, have contracted this terrible disease for which there is no cure. I say this on purpose to frighten you, Miss Poppy, because you take these things too lightly. If you can imagine one of your friends, one moment perfectly hale and hearty and intelligent, then suddenly becoming a drooling madman, never to return to his normal state of mind, you would probably stop like me and think twice before taking on one of these pariah dogs."

But I was undeterred, and Foxy, as I called him, was a great joy on the journey home and gave us such fun and amusement, that even Uncle Pop enjoyed playing with him too. By the time we arrived back we were both firmly attached to him.

He settled down well in Rangoon and was growing up into quite a good-looking little dog. We were devoted to each other; he was by no means the ugly scarecrow that Uncle Pop had prophesied, and was well behaved, too. One could hardly believe after a few months that he could ever have been a stray from a jungle village. Only the Burmese servants, knowing his background, always treated him with utter contempt, though he did his best to try to win their hearts.

I was upstairs changing one morning after our ride when I heard a shrill unearthly wail coming from the garden. I went to the verandah and saw Foxy dashing up the garden towards the house, then going round and round in circles as if he were having a fit.

Uncle Pop had seen him too, and called up from below, "Stay where you are, Miss Poppy, and shut the door. Your dog has gone mad."

I was horrified, and felt helpless, watching the poor little creature; he certainly looked possessed, but after a few minutes he calmed down and seemed to become normal again.

"Perhaps it is only hysteria or a fit, after all," said Uncle Pop.

We sent for the vet. The dog was trembling and sweating with fright when he came, but seemed to be recovering, and to my joy hysteria only was diagnosed. A sedative was given, and the vet said he was sure all would be well, but that he would call again next day. The servants were not convinced, however, and wouldn't go anywhere near the puppy; they went about all day looking ill at ease, and muttering, "It's a youdi quai"(mad dog).

Uncle Pop and I felt happy about it, as we had seen the vet put his hand right into Foxy's mouth and he would certainly not have risked touching the deadly rabies saliva had he not felt quite certain.

That evening I went to a party. I tied the dog to the foot of the bed, with a cushion to sleep on so that he should be comfortable and not stray away while I was out.

I came in late, and found the room in utter chaos—the cushion was in shreds, chewed-up bits of matting were all over the room, and I could not see Foxy anywhere. I found him cowering under the bed, heavy saliva drooling from his mouth.

Eventually I managed to get him into a corner of the room without touching him—I was beginning to doubt the vet's judgment and felt terribly worried.

When he came early next morning, however, he still said he was sure it was not rabies. But Uncle Pop put his foot down and insisted that to be on the safe side Foxy must be sent away for observation. Luckily, we were within reach of the only Pasteur Institute in the country, and I took him there.

On the way, the puppy had another severe fit, and it was all I could do to prevent him leaping from the car. At the Institute, he was put in a wired pen and looked most forlorn and wretched—I hated leaving him there, and told the man in charge I would be back to see him later.

In the evening, I found Foxy cowering in the back of his cage, obviously suffering, and he did not recognise me at all. It was more than I could bear, and I felt the time had come to ask them to put him out of his misery.

It was routine in these cases for a post-mortem examination of the brain to be made, and a message came through the next morning that the little dog had had rabies.

I was tremendously shocked, and Uncle Pop was thoroughly shaken, too, and kept asking me whether the dog had licked me or not. In order to ease his worry, I told him I was sure that Foxy had not done so—all I could think of was the sorrow of losing my little dog.

But Uncle Pop, I could see, was deeply worried—he kept staring at me in a peculiar way and asked me several times if I had any scratches or small abrasions anywhere on my arms or legs that the saliva could have got into. I didn't think I had, but when I looked I found I had quite a number of tiny scratches that I would never have noticed in the ordinary way.

I woke up next morning in the early hours—that time when everything is out of balance and the smallest anxieties can become overbearing. I thought of what Uncle Pop had told me in the jungle about the horrors of rabies; and the wonderful and awful description of hydrophobia in Axel Munthe's book, *San Michele*, came back to me and terrified me.

By six o'clock in the morning I not only felt there was a possibility I was going to get this awful disease, but every probability. I was tired out and exhausted by the time I got up. I was certain the puppy had licked me all over, as puppies always do, and with these small open scratches on my skin, how could I fail to get rabies, with all the awful consequences?

In the cold light of day, when I was up and about, all these worries seemed ridiculous, but as time went on I found my mind harping back to it again and again. As for Uncle Pop, he seemed to have forgotten all about it for the moment, and had reverted to his usual preoccupied self.

When he came in that evening, however, he took one look at me and said, "Good God, girl, you look a wreck—you have been worrying yourself about this damn rabies. Come along, I am going to take you straight away to the Pasteur Institute to have the antidote treatment. As a matter of fact, I have been going through a bit of hell about you, too, but one has to weigh these things up. What's most important is to prevent people getting into a state of panic about themselves, but I can see that that is what you are now in, so let's get cracking."

How I regretted that pup by the time I had finished the fourteen giant injections—one every morning into my stomach. By the fourteenth day I felt there was no room for any more; apart from everything else, they had a depressive effect and made me feel miserable.

Uncle Pop had his own psychiatric treatment—he insisted I keep up my long daily rides with him no matter how rotten I felt.

Towards the end of the fortnight, I told him that the doctor had said that I must keep quiet. "Oh, those doctors, they are all for your giving way. That never does anyone any good," he replied.

I was left wondering, as I had so often done before, whether he lived in a closed world of his own with little feeling for anyone else, or whether in his own gruff way he was really trying to do what he thought was best for other people.

As for myself, when all this was over I could only look back with deep relief and thankfulness. If this had had to happen at all, at least it had happened here in Rangoon where antidote treatment was available. If the puppy had caught rabies only a few weeks earlier in the jungle, we should not have been able to reach help in time.

*　　*　　*

We had been back about six months when rioting broke out in Rangoon. Burma was going through a period of depression and the Indian was regarded as the despoiler. Uncle Pop was fearless in most things; the fighting in the streets became quite fierce at times, but he never missed going to the office, and always carried a loaded revolver with him.

"I'll shoot the bastards if they attempt to get me," was his pet remark. "I'll cut their livers out and slide on them."

He represented the ruling power, and none must thwart him; the riots were not anti-British and he really had no occasion to defend himself, but he was in his element.

He had to leave Rangoon for a few days on business while the riots were on, and he was worried whether I would be all right in the bungalow alone, as the servants slept in their quarters some little way away from the house.

"I think you should have a gun," he said. "I am taking my shot-gun with me, so I will leave you the big game rifle and a couple of cartridges—better keep it by your bed at night."

The thought of using a rifle worried me much more than any rioters, although he had taught me the bare rudiments of shooting.

I had come in late from a dance one night soon after he had left when in the distance I heard some shots. Rather sleepily I decided I had better load my gun, which was on the table by the bed. I did not sleep very well, and later on started thinking about the safety catch which I had been warned was very stiff.

I don't know what possessed me, but for some unknown reason I decided I had better get out of bed and make sure that I could move it. One thing I did know about the gun was that it must be kept pointed downwards. I was careful to do this, pointing it through the french windows towards the open verandah.

But by mistake I pressed my finger on the trigger when pushing the safety catch. There was a terrific explosion, and the recoil knocked me backwards—the room was full of smoke and the smell of gunpowder. I replaced the big game rifle on the table, trembling at the knees and feeling an absolute fool.

I could just imagine that the next thing would be that all the local residents would come running to see what was the matter; and I went out onto the verandah and strolled up and down, pretending that the noise had not come from our house. I was just in time to see the night watchman and the gardener running hard across the compound in the opposite direction, as if there were an army of devils after them. They would have been as much good for protection as a sick headache.

Next morning I found an enormous hole blown in the cement floor of the verandah. I didn't know how I was going to face Uncle Pop, but I telephoned a very good friend of mine in the Public Works Department and told him the whole story, and he promised he would have the hole filled in and clean the rifle for me, and that nobody would be any the wiser.

Just as I had expected, kind friends and neighbours living near had heard the noise, and arrived while I was having breakfast to say that the fighting had come very near during the night, and wouldn't I feel happier to move over and live with them until my uncle returned? I think they all admired me very much when I said I was quite all right and wasn't in the least afraid.

Three months went by and I had completely forgotten this ridiculous incident. Uncle Pop was planning another tour and he came to me one morning, saying, "San Baw tells me he gave you two cartridges with that rifle when I went away, but when you handed it back there was only one—what happened to the other?"

I shamefacedly told him—and waited for an angry tirade —but he just put back his head and roared with laughter, saying, "It's the first time I have ever heard of anyone trying to shoot bison in the suburbs of Rangoon."

I had a feeling he was quite proud that I had managed to fire a gun at all, even if I had only done in the verandah.

Chapter VI

MEETING IN THE JUNGLE

WHAT stranger place could there be to meet one's destiny than the depths of the Burma jungle, yet this is what happened to me. I was on another tour with Uncle Pop, and we were camped in a clearing surrounded by gigantic trees, wonderfully green and cool after the long tramp of the day before.

Uncle Pop had gone upstream, fishing for mahseer. I had made some excuse to stay behind, as by now I felt I knew only too well all the trends of his conversation, and fishing bored me anyway. I longed to have a peaceful moment to lie down and read my book. I loved these times alone in the quiet of the jungle. Luckily one of the good things about Uncle Pop was that he hardly ever seemed to know or notice whether I was with him or not, which saved me from any feeling of guilt.

How restoring it was to lie in the long canvas chair at the entrance to my tent, angled so that a shaft of strong sunlight slanting through a gap in the thick leaves overhead made a warm beam right onto my legs. As I lay half drowsing, the gurgle of the jungle stream close by was beginning to lull me to sleep. But I was brought out of my reverie again and again by a pair of gibbon apes somewhere out of sight, way up in the very top of the trees, making their whoo-whoo calls to each other.

I had finally fallen into quite a deep sleep, when I woke up with a start, feeling that someone was about. I thought I

44

could hear the sound of voices, but this was most unlikely. After a moment or two I was sure, and got up off the chair, wondering who on earth it could be.

I walked a little way across the clearing, and then saw two men coming through the trees towards me. The taller of the two was fair and looked like an Englishman; the shorter one was undoubtedly a Burman, and was carrying a gun. We would go for days and weeks on these jungle treks without meeting anybody, and had certainly never met anyone just by chance like this.

My face must have fallen and I looked so completely non-plussed that as they came closer I saw that the taller man was smiling, and I remember immediately noticing what a kindly humorous face he had.

"Have we startled you out of your wits?" he said. "Don't be frightened, we are not jungle bandits. My name is Jim Williams, and I am a Forest Manager, doing a tour of this area. As a matter of fact, we had planned to camp in this clearing where you now are." He said that he had come across Uncle Pop fishing further upstream, and had been told by him to come on into our camp. "But he never told me I was going to find you here," he added.

I thought how like Uncle Pop to have forgotten my exis-tence—all the same, I was delighted to see someone young and so obviously lively. He started to tell me about his Alsatian dog which I had just noticed at his heels.

"I'm afraid I have the most unfriendly dog in the world," he said. "She is extremely good-natured, but like all Alsatians is very single-hearted and I can't make her take any interest in anybody but me."

I couldn't help laughing, for as he was talking the dog came bounding forward, pushing herself against my legs, obviously asking to be made a fuss of.

"Do you mean I ought to be careful about touching her?"

"I simply don't know," he said, "as I have never seen her do this before to anybody."

This of course pleased me enormously, and at once I felt more at home with her and her master—I began secretly to hope that Uncle Pop's fishing would keep him occupied for a long time.

The Burmese servant had wandered off, and we sat down together to have a drink.

"I still haven't told you who I am," I said. "I'm Mr. Hopwood's niece."

"I don't care who you are," he replied. "It's just the greatest fun to be sitting down here having drinks, so unexpectedly, alone with a pretty girl. I don't think I've ever done such a thing in my life before in the middle of the jungle."

He told me how he had been out here for about ten years, working for the Bombay Burmah Teak Corporation, and that his home and family were in Cornwall. I don't think either of us realised how long we had been sitting talking, when we were suddenly surprised by the clap-clap sound of elephant bells close at hand.

"Those must be my camp elephants arriving," he said. "I had better go and tell the men that you have bagged our site, but that your uncle said there would be room enough for both camps."

The leading traveller then came into view—a magnificent male elephant with gleaming tusks. He was followed by about fourteen others, of various sizes. I was so obviously interested that Jim said, "Like to come over and have a look, and I'll tell you about them."

We walked across the clearing. "The fine chap leading," said Jim, "is normally a 'worker,' not a 'traveller', but he's convalescing. He had a breast strap rub causing a boil that had to be cut, but he's nearly ready to go back to work now."

He went across to the elephant and spoke a few words in Burmese to him. "I never go up to an elephant without talking to him," he said. "They need to be spoken to more than any other animal." He patted the giant beast who seemed to understand what was wanted; without any command, he raised his trunk and let Jim examine where the hurt had been. There was little sign of any trouble now except a longish white scar. Jim felt this and, looking up at the man on his head, said, "No trouble here, he's almost ready to go back to dragging again."

Next in the line were three females; he explained that they were elderly—probably between fifty and sixty years old—and ending their working days doing light jobs. Then came the youngsters, their ages varying from twenty-one down to eight—the latter were small, round tubby animals, carrying very little in the kahs on their backs. They were giving chirrups and squeals of joy at the thought of being unharnessed and freed to stuff themselves with food again. They were on the move all the time exploring with their trunks—a healthy elephant is never still.

Jim told me that these young ones were now being used as travellers to carry the baggage, as they had lately left school and must be taught something new all the time. He said that they were just like children, all with completely different characters. I was so amused at the idea of an elephant going to school that I thought he was pulling my leg.

He noticed my doubtful look and said, "I'm not joking—it's true. At six years old an elephant starts being a nuisance to its mother and everyone else around. It is weaned, and it is time to start training it. What we in the teak company call 'the School' is really only a clearing in the jungle where the oozies, or elephant men, bring all mother elephants in the district with calves of six years old and upwards. In this clearing we build what are known as 'crushes'—these are small triangular enclosures made of logs, the whole thing being just big enough to hold the calf. The wide end is left open for the baby elephant to enter. Sometimes he will do so without any bother at all, the enticement being a large bunch of bananas, or a stick of juicy sugar cane. Other times he refuses to enter on his own and has to be gently pushed and coaxed all the time by tempting morsels held in front of him. Very often his

47

mother, who has stood by watching the whole operation without making any fuss, gives him a final push from behind. Having done so, she then turns away as if to say, 'You're out of the way at last, and the term can go on for forty years for all I care.'

"Once he is in, he cannot hurt himself when he heaves and shoves, as the whole contrivance has been covered in slippery grease made from the melted-down fat of a bear or a wild pig. To start with, he is a bit obstreperous, and so while he is in the crush the calf is never left alone. He is being taught something all the time, and as this can only be done by kindness, a lot of patience and coaxing are needed. However, he is very quick to learn, and at the end of only twenty-four hours will let a boy sit on his head, and will understand and obey the commands to get up and sit down."

I was fascinated by all this, and sensed at once that these elephants meant something out of the ordinary in this man's life. I should have liked to have heard more, but at this moment Uncle Pop strolled into camp. He was in a very good humour, the reason being a large fish, a nine-and-a-half-pound mahseer carried on a stick by the Burman behind him.

"Put up a wonderful fight," he said. "I see you two have met—glad to have you eat with us this evening, Williams." With that he wandered off to his tent for a bath and change.

That evening, seated round an enormous log fire, we had to listen to Uncle Pop's time-worn shikar stories of tiger shoots and bison hunts. I thought he would never stop.

At last he made a move and said, "I'm off to bed, good-night both of you."

We talked on late, and Jim told me how from very early days he had been a great animal lover and how during the last ten years he had made a very special study of the elephants and their habits while he worked with them. As a result he had now been chosen to go off to the Andaman Islands where the Bombay Burmah Teak Corporation were thinking of opening up new timber forests. They wanted him to find out if there was sufficient fodder there to support a working herd.

Elephant Bill

Uncle Pop

Jim's leading travelling elephants
coming into camp

It always seemed to happen that whenever I had felt a special interest in anybody, fate seemed to intervene and for some reason or other they had soon to be moving on. Even when we were in Rangoon, once or twice when I had been getting on rather well with someone, Uncle Pop had announced that we were about to go off on an expedition. I must admit that none of these former attachments had been very serious, and I had not minded overmuch.

But I was surprised, almost angry with myself, to find how miserable I felt at the thought that this young man, whom after all I had only known for one day, was going away and that I should probably never see him again. I comforted myself that when daylight broke I would most likely feel quite differently about it all.

I think Uncle Pop was amazed how eager I was to go with them next morning when they went off together on a tour of inspection. Jim's dog, Molly, was very much on my side; she made a tremendous fuss of me the whole day, and even came and lay across my feet when we stopped for a rest.

That evening we fed in Jim's camp. Uncle Pop was not to have his favourite meal, which usually consisted of tinned soup, tinned vegetables and tinned fish, which he liked unadorned. Instead we had a meal which I found it almost impossible to believe could have been produced in the jungle: chicken soup, roast duck, green peas and beautifully creamed duchess potatoes, followed by fresh mushrooms on toast.

When I asked Jim how he got this delicious meal together, he just winked and said, "Oh, Fortnum's delivered it from London this afternoon," and that was all I was able to find out.

At nine-thirty sharp, Uncle Pop got up as usual to go to bed. Jim was moving off the next day, and he and I stayed talking by the fire.

Sitting in the jungle by the light of the huge glowing logs at this time of the evening warmed and relaxed one's body and one's spirit, and made one long for good conversation—something I had never been able to have with Uncle Pop.

With him I could only try to be a good listener. Jim must have realised this, because he led me on and at least made a good pretence of being interested in all my outpourings. I did not have to pretend anything with him, as everything he said interested me and he was full of humour.

Suddenly Molly jumped to her feet, her hair bristling all down her back. She sprang across to Jim's side.

"I think she must have heard a leopard or a tiger," he said. "Even the scent is sheer terror to a dog."

We stayed quite still, and listened. Coming from the stream below we heard a sort of muffled cough, then footfalls surprisingly heavy, like those of a large man padding along. Molly was the only one who was really frightened; we knew that all wild animals instinctively keep away from a fire. Although Jim told me how he had once been sitting just as we were now and a leopard had taken a flying leap between him and the fire in an unsuccessful attempt to seize his dog, but this was a most unusual thing to happen.

Jim put out his hand to soothe Molly, and she looked up and thumped her tail on the ground. I then asked him if young elephant calves were ever attacked by tigers, and he told me that in the wild when a mother elephant is about to have a calf the herd find a safe place for her, usually at the fork of a stream. They then trample down all the long grass and undergrowth until they have made a large circular area, worn quite bare and hard as a rock with their stamping.

Usually near the chosen place is a big tree, heavily hung with creepers, whose thick stems at the base provide a sort of protective natural stall. The calf is born here, and the herd, having formed themselves into a circle round mother and baby, spend the night trumpeting and banging on the ground with their trunks to frighten away any marauding animals.

They stay here like this for about twenty-four hours until the baby is strong enough to move off with them. But it is always a mystery, Jim said, how the baby travels for the first few days, for its tracks are rarely found. It almost seems as though at this early stage the mother may carry it in her trunk, as the newly born calf is very small—only just over two feet high.

I wanted to know what happened with elephants in captivity. He told me that with the domesticated animal the herd instinct is lost, but over the years they had thought out and developed another way of protecting their young from tiger attack.

"We call this the 'Aunty system'," he said. "The first signs, and usually the only way we have of telling that an elephant is in calf, is when two females form a friendship. They will feed together and become almost inseparable—in fact the oozies never know which animal is the one in calf till probably the last weeks of a twenty-two-month pregnancy. This way, the newly-born calf is doubly protected."

Even so, he told me, losses among their calves were very heavy, whereas in the wild he doubted if there were any losses at all.

I couldn't believe that a tiger could carry away a baby elephant. Jim laughed, saying that it would only be like a savoury to a tiger—just mushrooms on toast. "He is quite capable of dragging a fully grown bullock he has killed, and can even jump the height of a five-bar gate with his kill."

All this time, Molly had looked miserable and ill at ease. She knew there had been a tiger around, and did not feel happy enough to settle down again. Jim held her head in his hands and, looking straight into her face, said, "It's all right, old girl—he's gone long ago." I could see there was a great bond between these two.

"What are you going to do with Molly when you go off to the Andamans?" I asked.

"I think that's about my biggest worry at the moment," he said. "Living as I do, for months on end alone in the jungle with this dog as my only companion, we have got so attached and dependent on each other's company that I don't want to be parted from her, but I can't take her with me and she would hate to go to anyone else."

"She doesn't seem to dislike me too much," I said.

"That doesn't mean you're trying to say you would take care of her for me, does it?" he asked. "That would solve everything."

I felt it would solve something for me, too—it would be a link with him.

We had both been shy, of course, but even at this first meeting the more Jim talked the more his tremendous zest for life came over to me. Despite a happy-go-lucky and easy manner, he immediately gave a sense of solidarity and strength, and inspired a deep trust that awoke something in me and disarmed me. Above all, one had the feeling that here was a man with faith in other people and faith in himself.

He obviously enjoyed telling me about his life and his animals, about the jungle and about his elephants, more so perhaps because these things were close to my heart too. But I wanted to hear more about him himself, and it was time to say goodbye.

I think we both secretly knew that within a short time some sort of unbreakable link had grown between us. It was a miserable feeling that he was now going so far away, but I was thankful he was leaving Molly with me. She was so much a part of him that I felt she would be a kind of hostage.

Chapter VII

HAPPY VOYAGE

In spite of all Uncle Pop's eccentricities, the trip had been full of interest. I had thoroughly enjoyed it and would have been sorry to be returning to the city again had I not known that Jim would be spending a week in Rangoon before going off. I was secretly hoping we might meet, and I put all my faith in Molly. I knew that he would want to know how she was getting on.

The jungle lost much of its thrill for me after Jim had gone, though this time I felt that I had a bit of an ally in Uncle Pop as I had heard him asking Jim to be sure and look us up before he sailed for the Andamans. Jim was a good listener, which suited him, and although I got impatient with the interminable fishing stories, patience this time might be well worth while. I knew that the more Uncle Pop got to know and like Jim, the more we were likely to see of him.

Back in Rangoon I waited anxiously for the telephone to ring. After a few days I began to lose hope and think he had forgotten both Molly and me.

One evening, as I came in before dinner, Uncle Pop met me in the hall. "Oh, by the way, Miss Poppy, that chap Williams has been on the phone enquiring about the dog—he wondered about coming round to see it. I told him I thought it would only unsettle the dog if he came round—much better if he kept away."

I couldn't say a word, and rushed upstairs and banged the door after me. Pacing round the bedroom, I felt I could have killed Uncle Pop.

After about a quarter of an hour I heard him calling my name and felt so irritated that I pretended not to hear. But he came upstairs and knocked at my door.

"You're an impatient creature," he said. "You never listen when I am talking, or let me finish."

This was the last straw—hadn't I spent my whole time out here doing just that?—*and* letting him finish.

"I was going to say, when you rushed out of the room, that Williams also wanted my advice about deep-sea-fishing tackle for the Andamans, and asked would it be possible for us to put Molly out of the way just while he came to see me? He said he had heard I knew more about it than anyone else out here, and he hadn't had any experience of it himself—so I asked the poor chap to dinner."

"Oh did you? When is he coming?"

"Tomorrow night," said Uncle Pop, and stumped down the stairs.

If I had felt cross with Uncle Pop, I now felt doubly furious with Jim; the dog—the fishing tackle—I was damned if I was going to ask Uncle Pop if he had asked after me.

Next evening, before dinner, I could hear them both talking away, deeply immersed. ". . . fish-hooks . . . traces . . . spoon bait . . ." and so on. What an impossible background this was for me to make any favourable impression on Jim—Uncle Pop would never allow me to get a word in edgeways. I was feeling altogether fed up.

As I went into the room he said, rather sarcastically, "Oh, here she is—punctuality never was one of her good points. Well, off you go, both of you, and have a good time."

"See you in the morning," he said, and strode off out of the room towards the dining room.

I felt very shy, and could not think what was happening. "I thought you had come to dinner, Jim," I said.

"Oh no, there must have been a muddle somewhere. I rang up yesterday to ask you to come out to dinner with me. Didn't your uncle tell you?"

54

"Oh, never mind," I said, "that's wonderful. I must just go and say goodnight to the old boy."

My heart went out to poor old Uncle Pop as he sat there, straight as a ramrod, alone at the dinner table. In the elation of the moment, I decided to give him a kiss. He looked puzzled and rather horrified—I never attempted it again.

All my worries were forgotten that evening, and Jim and I arranged to spend every minute of our spare time together for the remainder of that week.

The more I went about with him, the more I was drawn to his magnetic personality and tremendous sense of fun. We danced and laughed and talked about everything under the sun, and by the end of the week I knew I was in love with him and, what was more important, I felt that he loved me.

On that last evening together, when the thought of parting seemed unbearable, we agreed that if we both felt the same way when he returned in three months' time we would get engaged.

There were no mails from the Andamans and the weeks of silence that followed seemed endless. Then one morning an envelope arrived with the Singapore postmark—no letter inside, only an unsigned poem.

Mountains and woods and the winds that blow over them;
Meadows and downs, and the wild flowers that cover them;
Rocks and ravines, and the jungles that smother them;
    All these I love with a love that possesseth me,
    But more than all these I worship thee.

Sea and the shore, and the shells the gods squander there;
Corals and pools, and the wild things that wander there;
Silence and cares, and the thoughts that men ponder there;
    All these I love with a love that enchanteth me,
    But deeper in my depths springs love for thee.

This, Jim later told me, was taken from John Still's *Jungle Tide*, a book that he loved. I found out afterwards that a pilot of one of the Sunderland flying boats that were helping the expedition in their survey, had promised to post the envelope on his flight back.

My mind was fully made up long before the three months were over. Jim was due for leave in England after this assignment, and he wrote suggesting that I went home too, and that I should book a passage on the same ship as his.

I don't think Uncle Pop was a bit surprised when I told him I would be returning with Jim. He hadn't often approved of anyone I brought to his house, but with Jim it was different. "He really is a man," he said. This, coming from him, was high praise.

By the time we reached Colombo a fortnight later we were engaged. There could have been no more romantic place in which to celebrate.

The day we arrived Jim gave me a very beautiful sapphire ring—it has hardly left my finger since that day so many years ago. I grew to look on it as a talisman, and to think that he would always be safe while I wore it. Alas, time has proved me wrong—it was wishful thinking, as most talismans are.

* * *

On the way back he told me all about his home in the West Country. His father, a Cornishman, had been a mining engineer in South Africa, and he and Jim's mother had been caught in the Jameson Raid and had had to leave the country and all they possessed behind them.

They had temporarily taken a little house near St. Just in Cornwall, and although it was far too small his father had been so captivated by the wonderful sea views that he refused to move. He loved to tell everyone that he could see the beams of seven lighthouses from his bedroom window.

Jim had been born here, and he and his two brothers had had a wonderfully happy and carefree childhood, roaming the cliffs and getting to know every inch of the rocky coast. Even as very small boys they were quite at home in the sea, and could all three swim like porpoises.

He told me how when he had first joined the teak company and had had to live hemmed round on every side by trees in the jungle, it was wonderful to look forward to going home on leave to this Cornish countryside where there was not a tree to be seen—only the rugged moors leading right down to the wide open sea with its limitless space.

His mother loved Cornwall too, but she missed the mountains and trees of her native Wales. I think it was this mixture of Cornish and Welsh blood that made Jim so self-reliant and tough in many ways, and yet gave him his sensitive and sometimes almost psychic qualities. The toughness helped him to survive the hardships of jungle life; and the loneliness out there was relieved for him by his imaginative observation of all he saw, and his love of painting. Even on this voyage home, at each port we came to I would see him sitting, his sketching block on his knee and his paints beside him, blissfully lost to the world.

Later, when I met his mother, she showed me an album full of his sketches of the jungle. He had painted these for her all the time he had been away, and had slipped one into each of his weekly letters home. They had brought to her the colour and atmosphere of the places he had been in more vividly than any photograph could have done. One of them has been used for the jacket of this book.

It was she who told me how at the outbreak of World War I, Jim was seventeen and at the Camborne School of Mines. His elder brother Nick had joined the army, and he longed to do so too, but was too young. On his own initiative he decided to go and see the colonel of his brother's regiment. After much persuasion, he was allowed to join up, and was on active service in the Near East at seventeen and a half. He was away from home for over four years, finishing up in India and Afghanistan with the rank of captain.

At the end of the war, his father offered to set him up on a farm in Cornwall, but by this time Jim had been bitten by the wander bug. When he was in the East, he had met a

man who had given him an introduction to the Bombay
Burmah Teak Company, and he had set his heart on joining
it.

His mother and father were sad to let him go again so
soon, but he had always been determined and so at the age
of twenty-three he went off to his first job, as a Forest Assistant in Burma.

CHAPTER VIII

A NEW LIFE WITH JIM

WE were married at Evesham early in September, and set off on a motoring honeymoon. We made no plans as to where we were going, except that we had to end up in Liverpool in ten days' time when Jim's six months' leave was up and we were due to sail back to Burma.

Jim was extremely proud of the smart second-hand A.C. sports car he had just bought, especially as it had a racing clutch and made the most satisfying noise of power every time we moved off. I sat in her proudly, and as it purred along the car seemed as happy as ourselves.

It was one of those exhilarating English mornings when the sun chases the shadows over the hills. I had filled the pockets of the car with apples fresh picked from my grandmother's garden, and we munched these as we drove along— a happy, carefree start to twenty-six marvellous years together.

*   *   *

Jim had heard during this leave that he had a new posting, this time to Mawlaik on the Upper Chindwin River.

The forest manager from whom he would be taking over both the job and the house was a bachelor. "Don't expect the furnishings to be too grand," said Jim. "I don't imagine that he will have bothered much with those, but I do know the house itself, it's solidly built of teak and I think you will find it reasonable enough. Although you must not expect to find running water or electric fans, or anything much that helps when it gets really hot."

59

He told me that Aung Net, Po Lone and Joseph his cook—the three servants who had been with him before and who were all used to jungle life—would be coming there with us, and that they would be meeting us when we arrived in Rangoon.

Once on the boat, I plied him with questions about Mawlaik. He told me it was about five days up-country from Rangoon, on the banks of the Chindwin River and surrounded on three sides by the jungle so that it could not be reached by rail or road. It was in fact only approachable by river launch.

"I suppose most of the world," said Jim, "would think of Mawlaik as being 'at the end of back of beyond'. But in spite of its being so cut off and having so few amenities, men like me, who have lived for months in the jungle alone, come to think of it almost as a little city, so much do they look forward to going back there. The relaxation of being amongst company of one's own kind again is a luxury. And, my goodness, how some of them do beat it up when they return."

Jim went on to tell me how the native township was built on a fever-ridden piece of land lying between a marsh and the river, which when the rains came was usually flooded out. However, the houses of the British community—who were only about twenty in all and mostly employees of the Bombay Burmah Teak Corporation—were built on slightly higher ground set back well above water level.

"You will find nobody much over middle age in these up-country stations," he went on. "Mostly young men, in fact. In Mawlaik, as in all these places, they live in a little world of their own, but have managed to make a few amusements for themselves, such as a rough nine-hole golf course, a tennis court, a polo and football ground combined, and of course the usual club."

I asked if there were likely to be any other women there.

"That," said Jim, "we will have to wait to find out until we arrive."

We were to spend two nights in Rangoon en route, and when the ship docked, Aung Net, Po Lone and Joseph were waiting excitedly on the wharf to greet Jim. I recognised them at once from his descriptions. Aung Net, who had been with him all the time he had been in Burma, was dark-skinned for a Burman and very plain. Jim had originally picked him up as a ragged urchin in the jungle, and he had been with him ever since. He had a childish devotion for his master, and would have died for him—he was in fact once responsible for saving his life.

Some years before, they were in the jungle and Jim had been reprimanding an assistant servant for stealing. Without warning, the servant whipped out a dagger and lunged at him. Jim, who had boxed for the army, with one punch sent him reeling, but the tough little Burman, having spun completely round, came at him again still with the dagger in his hand, and this time the knife stabbed. Luckily, Jim still had the strength to get the Burman on the ground and hold him down. Aung Net, hearing the scuffle, came rushing up through the trees and was able to remove the dagger from the servant's grip—Jim was bleeding badly, and but for Aung Net's intervention, the incident might have had fatal results.

Joseph the cook was much older; he had a kindly face and grey hair. A little black fez hat sat on his head, and in all the years to come I don't think I ever saw him without it, either indoors or out. He was a Madrassi, but unlike the average Indian, who is very prone to malaria, he did not mind going into the jungle. He also had been with Jim many years.

Po Lone had only been with Jim three years, and did not mean as much to him as the other two. He was a townee, and though a well-trained servant, was inclined to be slick and clever—but I knew I should have to depend on him a good deal as he was the only one who could speak English and my Burmese was very weak.

Mawlaik had no shops, only a native bazaar, so we had to buy all our stores here in Rangoon. We were both lighthearted and inexperienced in the art of housekeeping, and heedlessly spent a small fortune. In fact, it took more than a year to pay for our purchases, and in the end many of the things we bought were never eaten.

Jim had as great a weakness for shopping as I, and he told me that when he had been on his own in the jungle, he would often amuse himself when bored by having masses of catalogues sent out, and ordering all sorts of useless things from them.

There had been one particular occasion when, as a young man spending his first year in the jungle, his love of catalogues and his generous disposition might have got him into serious trouble.

It was Christmas and he was alone in camp—day-dreaming of a white one in England. Feeling gift-minded, he was amusing himself by hunting through a catalogue, which in this case was from a large general store in Calcutta. He came to a page headed:

BLANKETS

Best Italian Goat Wool latest import from Italy in all colours Ten Rupees each. Special terms for quantities of ten for ninety Rupees.

It sounded a bargain. He decided he would give his servants and camp followers a present of one each, and if there were one or two over they would be useful for any sick people he might come across.

The ten blankets duly arrived. They were rough and gay— it didn't matter whether they were fast colours or not, for a jungle Burman never washed a blanket anyway. After all, dirt meant warmth and the baking sun would keep it vermin-free.

His servants were delighted with them. During the cold nights of the jungle open season camp fires died early. The Burmans huddled into those blankets and slept like mummies, instead of crouching round the embers half asleep.

It occurred to Jim then that perhaps beri-beri—a disease prevalent amongst his oozies and their wives—might be partly due to lack of warmth, for they were already supplied with food containing the right vitamins. He longed to afford five hundred blankets for them. But at that time he was only a junior—his pay was modest and he knew he could not get credit. He wondered if he dare order them and take a chance that the oozies would pay him back, if in the meantime he used some of the funds in his charge. He risked it and wrote for five hundred—an outlay of 4,500 rupees.

He was miles away in the forest when they arrived in bundles by special runners—cash on delivery. He paid the money from his cash box feeling as if he had robbed a bank, and replaced it with an I.O.U. for "Blankets 4,500Rs".

Loneliness can increase worry to panic. By issuing the blankets he gave sleep to five hundred oozies but robbed himself of sleep for a month. He toured from camp to camp in the usual way to settle wages, but on this trip he had to ask each oozie to accept a blanket as part of his pay. He half expected a riot, but there was none and by the end of the tour he was solvent again.

Jim spent the following Christmas with the local Goanese jungle doctor and told him the story. Strangely enough, this time the doctor had none of his usual gruesome tales to tell of beri-beri in the elephant camps, of women with swollen breasts split like ripe tomatoes, such as he had had in the past. It seemed a miracle—there had not been a case of beri-beri for months.

Blankets became an issue to all elephant oozies within a few years, and beri-beri became conspicuous by its absence.

*　　*　　*

Two days later we boarded the Mandalay mail train for the second stage of our journey. The first-class compartments in which we were to travel were comfortable and well ventilated —the third class were very different; there were no fans and the heat must have been suffocating. The Indians and Burmans were cramming themselves into the carriages, and in fact lots of them preferred to climb up and lie on the roof, travelling that way. As the train departed, there were hundreds of pairs of dark-skinned feet protruding from all the windows—it was the only way of keeping cool.

Once outside Rangoon, the train passed through acres and acres of flat baked-up paddy fields and here and there one could see the ubiquitous buffalo wallowing in some muddy pond. We crossed many bridges which had no side railings, and the train sometimes seemed to be suspended in space hundreds of feet over the ravine of some dried-up river bed.

As we went by small villages, where all the houses were perched on stilts, we could see the little naked fat brown Burmese children crawling perilously up improvised ladders to get into their homes.

Habitations became fewer and fewer, and as the jungle crowded more thickly down on to the track the train began to go slower. The driver was constantly on the lookout for any saing, bison or elephants who might have strayed onto the line. We passed through dense bamboo forest interspersed with trees of magnificent height and girth, through which small flocks of jade-green parrots flashed their way. We could even hear their squawking cries above the grinding of the wheels and the answering calls of the monkeys hidden in the leaves.

Our long train journey through Burma ended at Monywa, and here we boarded the Bombay Burmah launch for our journey up the Chindwin. She was a beautiful little miniature showboat painted white with a black stack, and lay anchored beneath a deep embankment among long lines of other small craft, rafts and country boats tied up at the river's edge.

It was just before darkness fell, and the palm trees on the high foreshore were already beginning to stand out as black silhouettes against the rosy red light cast on the river by the setting sun. Looking across the wide reach of water to the green trees on the other side, one's eye was carried far beyond, into the blues and purples of the distant hills slowly merging into the evening haze.

As we clambered rather perilously down the steep gang-

Baby elephant doing its first travelling job

Young elephant
in training crush

Still a bit uncertain o
the 'hmit' position

plank, Jim turned to me, saying, "This is the part of the journey we are going to enjoy most. With any luck at all, we shall be the only passengers on this little boat—and for three days we'll be able to imagine we're sailing up the Chindwin on our own private honeymoon yacht. After that it will be back to work for me and unpacking and settling down for you, so we might as well make the most of it."

We looked back, and saw Molly dithering at the other end of the plank, gazing down into the water and afraid to cross. We couldn't help laughing at her—she looked deeply offended, as she sat down on her tail, utterly dejected with her ears held back.

"It's the height that's worrying her," said Jim. "She doesn't really mind the water."

For about ten minutes he stood on the plank, cajoling and persuading, but it was no good—much to her displeasure, he finally had to pick her up and carry her across the plank, which swayed about as she kicked protestingly against him. Once on board she settled down happily.

"We're out of luck," said Jim, as he came into our cabin a little later. "There's one other passenger on this boat— someone I know—a Forest Manager called Jock Lifton, going up as far as Mingin."

"What's he like?" I asked.

"Oh, he's all right—you'll see for yourself," Jim answered.

That night, because of the heat, our camp beds were set up on the fore deck of the boat, and it was beautiful out there in the warm air, listening to the calls of the local boatmen shouting to each other in the dark as they tied up their craft for the night. The romance of it all was only slightly spoiled by the fact that we were both encased in a large netting cage to keep the mosquitoes out—and felt slightly as though we were in a meat safe.

Jim was asleep. Suddenly the netting near my head was pulled aside and I saw a man with a fat round greasy face peering at me through thick glasses.

"Who is this caught in the butterfly net?" he said, breathing alcohol into my face. "By God, it *is* a butterfly, too," he drawled, as he leaned over my pillow.

Jim was out of bed at the double. "Come on, Jock, come along, old chap," he said, leading him away. "I'll see you into bed."

So this was to be our honeymoon companion. I liked him even less the next morning, as he sat leaning halfway across a small table near the ship's rail, glass in hand, already rather drunk. A small terrier was sitting at his side, exactly like himself, with the same drooping expression and goggle eyes— it looked as if it had had a jolly good swig too.

"Have you ever seen such a washed-up looking pair?" I said. "Thank God he's not going to Mawlaik."

"No, never—but one has to have more tolerance than usual out here," said Jim, "for such characters as old Jock. I knew him as an eager young chap when he first came out, about eight years ago, just down from university—quite brilliant, with a double tripos. No one really knew why he had chosen the tough and lonely life of a Forest Assistant in the jungle, and quite early on we could see it was getting him down. But he had more determination than most and wouldn't give up.

"He started to drink, to forget his loneliness—now he really is lonely, sozzled most of the time, always miserable and no company for anybody except that pathetic dog which never leaves his side. Even that has grown equally miserable by the look of it. What puzzles me is how he manages to run his forest —but he must be able to somehow or other, as he still holds the job down. You'll come across others like him, too, in this country, turning either to drink or to women for solace— sometimes they mix the two—and then, heaven help them."

We steamed up-river from Monywa next morning, passing occasional villages; some coming down to the river's edge and encircled in palm trees, others set back in the forest, and we only knew they were hidden there by the dazzling white or gleaming gold pagodas rising above the trees, or perched on seemingly inaccessible promontories.

The river narrowed, and widened again as we chugged along, steaming sometimes through deep gorges of sheer red sandstone cliffs surmounted by thick tropical vegetation, and other times opening out again into peaceful stretches nearly a mile wide, where we could lie back in the cool breeze, resting our eyes on the mountains rising blue in the distance.

We lay side by side in long deck chairs, lulled by the never ceasing rhythmical chant of the Indian crew as they took soundings with bamboo poles—"Ek bam mila nahin—Hath kum do bum"—they sang these words back and forth to each other the whole way up the river; it was hypnotising in its monotony.

We didn't expect to see Jock Lifton at dinner that night. He had been shut up in his cabin all through the heat of the day.

"He'll be dead out by now, I think," said Jim, "and we probably shan't see him again till he rolls down the plank to disembark at Mingin tomorrow."

But as we were speaking, he came up behind us. We were amazed at his changed appearance. There he was, shaved and bathed, dressed in fresh white duck trousers and open-necked shirt, with a smart black cummerbund round his waist. He made us both feel quite shabby. True, he was swaying a little, but he had evidently made a tremendous effort. He talked quite well at dinner, and Jim even managed to make him laugh. For a little while, the drooping corners of his mouth lifted and the bleary eyes almost sparkled.

Jim stayed up talking with him after I had gone to bed, till the early hours. "There's something thoroughly nice about old Jock, really," he said later, "and I think probably more than half his trouble is that his brain was altogether too good for the people he had to mix with out here, and no one really liked him because of it. We'll give him a jolly good send off anyway, when he goes ashore this morning."

We woke up to a tremendous chatter and bustle. The boat had drawn alongside at Mingin and all the villagers had come down to have a look at us. Some of them were coming on board to sell their sweet limes, oranges and bananas. The array of bright cotton skirts, vying with each other in brilliance, was a patchwork quilt of colours.

After an hour we were due to sail on again, but still Jock Lifton had not appeared, and the Indian serang sounded the ship's siren once or twice to hurry him up. His servants had already taken his luggage off and it was piled up on the sandy bank beside the river, with the little dog sitting stiffly like a china ornament on top of it.

Eventually he came shuffling and swaying along the deck, still in his bedroom slippers, hair unbrushed and glasses awry. His vest was tucked into a crumpled pair of wide-legged magenta silk trousers, and he clung like grim death to a large iron-bound teak money-box which he held in his arms. Jim put out a hand to help him towards the gang-plank, but he shook him off.

Like a tightrope walker, he balanced himself down the plank with the box held out in front of him, stopping every few seconds to try to grab at his trousers, which seemed to be falling down. We expected to see him topple over into the water at any moment, but by some miracle he made it.

The crowd were enthralled and the children roared with laughter, but there was a gasp from the Burmese women when, as he started to climb the three stone steps onto the bank he raised one hand to wave goodbye to us, and his trousers fell right down round his ankles.

We steamed off up-stream, and as we rounded the bend in the river we saw him for the last time—sitting there only in his vest, still clinging to his box.

Chapter IX

A HOUSEHOLD ON THE TREK

W E were nearing the end of our journey, and I was glad to think that we would soon be seeing our future home. The little paddle boat gave two loud honks on its siren as we approached the Mawlaik jetty towards evening next day.

We anchored alongside a steep sandy bank overhung with dark evergreen trees. Perched on top was a row of little wooden shacks and beside them stood a bullock cart; this had come to carry our luggage. There was no other transport of any kind in this place.

After we had landed, we had about a mile to walk to the house. The red hard-baked stony road led us through the local bazaar—which consisted only of a line of rather fly-blown native owned wooden shops. When we came to the white painted gate and I saw our bungalow built of teak with its deep hanging eaves and verandah all round, I thought it was exactly as Jim had described it to me.

This was the first of many occasions in my life when Jim's descriptions had come to life, as it were. He had the ability to select with great awareness and observation all the salient features from anything he saw, and to give one a vivid picture alive with detail, which turned out to be absolutely accurate when one encountered it for oneself. It was this gift, I think, which enabled him to write so well.

The big open verandah was obviously used as a living-room— a few rather ancient cane chairs were set stiffly around a small table covered by what looked extraordinarily like a red bandana handkerchief full of holes. I noticed that all the table legs were placed in tin lids filled with kerosene to prevent the ants climbing up when food was around. The whole thing was bleak and uncared for.

All the essential furniture had been supplied by the firm—it was ugly and impersonal, but one could hardly blame the man who was handing over to us. After all, at least half the time he had been stationed here he would have been away from home, touring the jungle.

I wandered up the wide twisting teak staircase. It was beginning to get dusk, and I nearly jumped out of my skin when, gazing at me from a crack in the wood, was a huge lizard nearly a foot long. It was pink striped with black, and had round bulging eyes on swivels. I hadn't yet had a drink, so I knew it was true.

I called to Jim to come and look.

"It's all right, it's only a tauktè," he said. "It's quite harmless. You will get to know it and its friends well; there are quite a few of them living in the house and the servants love them, they think they are lucky."

I was to grow very familiar with the cry of these miniature dragons—rather like a cuckoo with a cork in its throat. They had suckers on their feet, and could walk on the ceilings with ease; I was told later that if they fell onto one's bare flesh, these suckers would stick like clamps and were terribly difficult to detach. I never experienced this calamity, but was never happy when having a bath to see a tauktè walking on the ceiling above me.

After we had gone to bed, Jim and I chatted over the day's events. It was good to be in our own home at last, and my sleep was sound.

Suddenly I was wide awake. I heard a metallic rattling coming from the verandah outside—it was brilliant moonlight and I could see, feeding from Molly's enamel dish, what looked like a gigantic rat. I leaned over and shook Jim.

"What's the matter?" he said sleepily. "Oh, that's only a bandicoot—I forgot to tell you about those, they won't do any harm—it's only come for the remains of Molly's dinner."

Even so, I was thankful I had Jim's company for my first introduction to up-country livestock. His calmness, plus the large mosquito net, did much to allay my fears.

After a while, all these things seemed quite commonplace. Besides the bandicoot and lizards, there were many creepy-crawly creatures to get used to; myriads of ants in the daytime, and at night, scorpions. These would venture out into the ring of light cast by the lamp to feed on the insects caught in its beam, looking rather like small crayfish, only shiny and black. They loved to hide under the pots and tins in the store cupboard, and one had to be careful when moving things—the sting in their tail could give one fever for a week.

Jim once, getting up hurriedly, forgot to shake his pants before putting them on—he was stung badly where it hurts most, and was quite ill as a result. If one of these creatures is stepped on or is injured, it will immediately finish itself off by curling its tail over and injecting itself with its own deadly poison.

It was November when we first arrived in Mawlaik, the loveliest time of the year in Burma, and the beginning of the cold season when every day is like perfect summer. Except at midday the sun was never over-powering, and at night it was even cool enough to have the joy of needing a blanket on the bed.

We left all our boxes from England unpacked, and concentrated, almost at once, on getting everything ready for Jim's first tour into the jungle to inspect his area. There were stores to be sorted, and other equipment to be checked.

How different my jungle clothes were from those I had worn with Uncle Pop. Jim had designed a special tunic for me, on the lines of an Australian bush shirt. It was made of soft grey washable material, belted and knee length, with four large pockets. It felt comfortable, and looked quite smart.

Jim's kit was much the same, except that it was khaki, and he wore shorts and golf stockings. His pockets were bulging with cigarettes, notebooks, pencils, and all the other paraphernalia needed on the march.

Our house was on the fringe of the jungle, so the elephants were able to come right into the compound; here they were loaded up from the back verandah. There were about twenty of them in all, varying in size, sex and age from the largest tusker to the flighty teenager, who was still learning and was only made to carry light weights. Each elephant had its individual load, which was kept the same so far as possible; for instance, one would have the tents and poles, another the beds and suitcases, and another the tables, chairs, wireless, etc.

Joseph the cook had one all to himself, loaded with his boxes of stores and cooking pots. Tied behind the lot were two plaited cane baskets containing live chickens and ducks, to be killed and eaten on the tour.

We were to be away for several months and so travelled as a complete household. There was little lacking in comfort either for us or our animals, who came with us. Molly walked alongside us, but Tigger, the Siamese cat, rode in style in her own basket on one of the elephants.

We set off at six-thirty in the morning, when it was cool, and marched for about four hours into the jungle before setting up our first camp. The elephants arrived soon after, and I loved watching them coming in and being unloaded.

They did not seem to be still for one moment, and were either scratching themselves with a bit of stick, blowing dust over themselves, or feeling round with the tips of their trunks for some titbit. We saw one pull up a tuft of grass and then very fastidiously flick it against its foreleg to remove the earth before putting it into its mouth. Another one went up to a tree and removed a creeper growing up it with the tiny finger-like tip of its trunk. First it gently shook it from the bottom to loosen it and then broke it off from the base with such delicacy and precision that the root was left undisturbed. Knowing an elephant's intelligence one felt that it was quite possible that all this care was taken so that the plant might grow again to provide more food for the following year.

The elephants were all unloaded in the 'hmit' or sitting position. They were halted a hundred yards or so from the camp so that the site would not be sullied in any way, and woe betide the oozie who forgot this order. Once unloaded, their fore feet were fettered and they were allowed to wander off at will to look for food. They could travel at quite a speed, even though hampered in this way.

Elephant men from the logging camp nearby had already prepared a camp site for us. The undergrowth had been cut down, and the ground bared of vegetation and swept clean. In the centre of the clearing, they had erected a little temporary *sabwe ohn* (or dining-room) for us. These little buildings were in themselves a work of art. Not a nail was used—they were beautifully constructed of materials gathered from the surrounding jungle. Rather like little open summer houses, their walls and eaves were woven in intricate patterns out of strips of bamboo. It never ceased to amaze me what trouble and artistry the builders put into the work, knowing it was probably only going to be used for one night.

In some districts it was the custom to weave a plaited bamboo floor resting on tree trunks about two feet high, on which our sleeping tent was then pitched. It was cleaner than the earth floor and was also a precaution against anyone entering at night without being heard, as the bamboo platform creaked with the lightest footfall.

Not that, as a rule, one had much fear of marauders, for in general the jungle Burman is a happy peace-loving individual. But as with everything else, exceptions had to be provided for. Bandits or dacoits were the exceptions in Burma. They roamed the jungle in small groups, out to get what they could, but were mainly interested in stealing guns or cash.

Jim never slept without a revolver under his pillow, which he could draw at a moment's notice. Sometimes he had to carry large sums of money—wages to be handed out, advances for contracts, for fire watching, etc. The money was kept in an iron-bound teak box always chained to his bed.

An Assistant we knew once had a rather horrifying experience with dacoits when camped in a very lonely part of the forest. He was sitting on the steps of his jungle hut with his shot-gun across his knee, already having been warned that there were bandits in the vicinity out to rob him. After a while, he saw two men approaching and shouted to them asking what they wanted. They seemed friendly enough, replying that they had only come to visit him.

"Why do you come with guns then?" was the Assistant's reply. "Put them down and I will talk to you."

At this, one of the dacoits raised his gun as if to fire, but the Assistant was quicker. He fired his own gun and both men dropped to the ground, killed with one burst of shot.

He was then filled with panic, picturing himself being arrested and tried for murder. After all, what proof had he that these men were bandits? He immediately had both corpses loaded onto an elephant, and did a two days' forced march into Toungoo, where he reported the matter to the police superintendent, and handed over the bodies. By this time they were in an advanced state of decay. Fortunately round the neck of one was a chain and locket, which gave a clue to his identity. He was a criminal on the wanted list for murder whom the police had been looking for for months.

Subsequently the Assistant received a letter from high authority congratulating him on his courage. It might have been a different story had there been no means of identification.

For protection from wild animals we always kept a large reflector lamp burning all night in the entrance to our tent. This was to protect our dogs as well. They are a specially juicy morsel easily snatched by a leopard, and many of them had met their end in the jungle through their masters not taking this precaution.

I remember how sad we were when a lovely black labrador dog we knew was lost in this way. A friend was in camp with his two dogs which he greatly loved—a brindle bull terrier and this labrador. They were all sleeping in a small jungle hut raised about ten feet from the ground on stilts. He felt at this height he would be safe enough without a light. But in the night he was wakened by a yelp and saw a leopard by the light of the moon flashing out of the hut with the labrador in its mouth.

He fired his revolver and sprang out of bed. It was too late—the leopard and dog had disappeared into the darkness. To his amazement, his bull terrier, forgetting the natural fear that a dog has for any of the larger cat tribe, had leapt the ten feet down to the ground, in hot pursuit. With all the courage in the world, and with so much noise and ferocity did he attack the leopard, that it dropped its prey and disappeared into the scrub. The labrador was so badly mauled, however, that it had to be destroyed—a great tragedy after such a show of bravery.

Jim was always impressing on his Assistants the importance of this light. Even so, some of them would not bother about it. One in particular nearly met his end as a result. He had gone to bed one moonlight night in his tent, when a wild elephant wandered near. Seeing the bulky shape in the half light, and evidently thinking it was a rival, it charged. As it tore through the tent with its tusks, the poor man was lifted, bed and all, and thrown into the jungle. His bed and much of his camp kit was smashed to smithereens.

He managed to clamber out of the wreckage, badly shaken but unhurt. Afterwards, he told us that he thought it was an earthquake that had hit him, and when Jim and I passed that way next morning and saw the wreckage, it certainly looked like it.

CHAPTER X

SOAPSUDS AND ELEPHANT SURGERY

AFTER the very austere and comfortless touring I had done with Uncle Pop, it was astonishing to me how quickly our servants set up camp and managed to make it homelike. As soon as we arrived one of them immediately shinned up the nearest tall tree to fix the wireless aerial, and within a few minutes we were listening to the chimes of Big Ben from London. This made us feel nearer home but when we thought of the thousands of miles between this jungle spot and Westminster we felt very far away.

Joseph set to, preparing his kitchen and Aung Net was busy making the tent habitable and later laying the table. I think he placed and replaced the knives and forks at least a dozen times before he was satisfied, all the time looking at me, grinning and waiting for approval. Another servant built a fire for the large kerosene tins, which, filled from the nearest stream, were used for heating our bath water.

When all was ready, we sat down to eat. Even in this out-of-the-way spot Joseph, after having done a march of from seven to ten miles, produced in a couple of hours a four-course meal equal to any in the best restaurant. Nothing was spoilt, and as I later found out to my delight he was able to cook a great variety of dishes such as pickled pork from jungle pig and roast saddle from barking deer. Added to this, Jim would sometimes shoot a jungle fowl, pheasant, or an occasional peacock.

Considering that his cooking stove consisted only of a twist of iron resting on two stones, and his oven was a disused kerosene tin, it was a complete marvel to me how he managed. I dread to think how any European would have got on in these circumstances. He even saw to it that we were given delicious fresh bread. How different it all was from Uncle Pop's dry as dust food.

Jim was always busy in camp—there was much office work to do, such as making working plans for the following year's extraction of teak, the placing of elephant camps, planning ahead for fire watchers to guard the logs in hot weather, and many other arrangements.

His Assistant had broadcast the news of his probable arrival weeks before and as a result, a procession of Burmans from the forest turned up to be interviewed. Each brought a small offering, bananas, sweet limes, or pineapples, and some brought half a dozen eggs on a plate.

These offerings became a regular feature of our tours and we later came to joke about these eggs—the donors passed through the servants' part of the camp on their way to present them to us. After each separate presentation, the eggs were removed by Aung Net, and I can still remember the not quite guileless look on his face as he carried them away. We often thought the same plate of eggs was used over and over again, judging by their staleness.

All this over, Jim came to where I was sitting. "Come on, Sue," he said, "the messenger has just been up to say that the elephants have been brought over from one of the elephant camps for me to inspect; they are being bathed just below here in a pool in the creek."

This was by far the best part of the day for Jim. Ever since he had been in Burma, elephants had been his greatest interest in life, and by now perhaps he knew more about them than anyone else in the country.

He had a passion for all animals. I have often heard him say, "There is more to be learnt of courage from an animal than in any other way." He was quite certain that he could never have fended for himself against the onslaughts of the jungle such as continual fevers, without having all round him the example of wild animal life—"and I think I have learnt this primarily from elephants and dogs," he would add.

The elephants were a wonderful sight; there they were, about a dozen of them, revelling in the water. Some of them were as reluctant to leave the pool as a child who, happily playing in his bath, is told it is time to get out. There were one or two females with very young calves, and these babies were quite adorable as they played games with each other and with their mothers in the river. Screeching with delight, they then chased each other out onto the sand, where they rolled on their backs just like puppies, their loose wrinkled skin covered with fine grey downy hair.

"Go wash an elephant if you want to do something big," the old song used to say—and these oozies who were scrubbing away at their elephants certainly had a big job on hand. Not an inch was left out and when they had finished one side they made them roll over onto the other. A particular sort of creeper which made a lather like soap was used for the washing and a coconut shell for the scrubbing. The elephants especially enjoyed the rough sensation that this gave them.

I noticed that some of them were syphoning the water into their trunks, opening their mouths wide and then blowing it down their throats. They repeated this over and over again.

"The elephant looks forward to his drink as much as to his bath, just like the old club member," said Jim, "except that these chaps have got an almighty thirst and can and will put back as much as eighteen gallons at a time. They are particular about their water being clean too, much preferring to drink from a limpid stream than a wide river. Perhaps this may have given rise to the ancients' belief that the female elephant would only drink from clear water because she liked to admire her reflection. Anyway we see to it that they get all the fresh water they want, and always pitch camp within reach of it. Wild elephants who have to find it for themselves are not always so fortunate."

The elephants emerged from the water a lovely blue-black colour, so different from the dusty grey they had been before going in. But how disheartening it must have been to the poor oozie, having taken all that trouble when the animal, as usually happened, on reaching the bank took up a trunkful of dusty sand and blew it all over itself. The elephants were often to be seen covering themselves in this way. The dust gave them protection against flies; for though their skin appeared tough it was in places quite delicate and an ordinary fly was able to draw blood from it.

Bathtime over, they were brought out of the river, some more willingly than others. It made us laugh to see the mothers taking the tails of some of their smaller children firmly in their trunks and then giving them a push against their fat little bottoms to help them up the steep bank.

Finally, they were all lined up for inspection. Every animal had its own log book in which its case history was carefully recorded. These were handed to Jim in turn as each elephant was brought up for him to look at. Faulty harness can cause severe rubbing, and he kept an eagle eye open for any sign of it.

He was horrified when he looked at the second animal and saw that it had a large swelling on its chest as big as a rugger ball. Jim rounded on the oozie, demanding an explanation, but none was forthcoming. He stepped forward and felt the swelling.

"This must be dealt with immediately, it's full of pus," he said.

His equipment was brought, a large razor-sharp bellied knife, about ten inches long, and a wooden mallet. He went up to the elephant, talking to it gently and firmly in Burmese, just as if it were another human being. Then, standing in front of it, he gave the order for it to raise its trunk. It lifted its massive head, and moving in beneath its gleaming tusks, Jim placed the knife in position, then with a swift blow of the mallet, the blade penetrated the thick hide making an incision several inches deep.

The elephant heaved and trumpeted with pain, but stood perfectly still, and I was filled with awe and admiration at this wonderful display of trust. Nearly a bucketful of pus poured from the wound, and the relief to the animal was obvious.

After giving it time to recover, Jim syringed out the wound with an antiseptic and applied a fly repellent. "Keep her tied up and hand feed her," he said to the oozie, "and I'll be back to see her tomorrow."

Next day the elephant was doing well, and three months later we heard it was quite fit and working again.

Chapter XI

THE HEART OF THE FORESTS

IT HAD been decided we were to move camp next day further into the jungle, to a place where Jim knew dragging was taking place.

Early in the morning he woke me. "I can hear the Kalaub bells of the elephants," he said, "they're coming into camp—time to get out of bed."

It could be very cold in the early morning, and I had little inclination to move out of the warm blankets. But I had to be out early, so that the tent could be packed up.

The wonderful beauty of the Burma jungle at dawn, with its poignant colouring will remain as a picture in my mind for always. The first light revealed the deepest of greens faintly tinged with pink—the soft mists clouding the river beds, and gradually disappearing as the sun rose.

In the background, the spirals and faint smell of wood smoke from the newly stirred camp fire gave a comfortable feeling that all was well. The call of the doves from the trees around, or the longer cry of the Burmese Imperial pigeon, were part of the early morning glory. Sometimes the occasional squeal of an elephant could be heard as he was being harnessed ready for the day's trip.

How exhilarating it was to sit, muffled up in a warm woolly sweater, sipping one's first cup of tea. I watched Aung Net standing by the camp fire, holding out Jim's vest and pants to warm—a service he never failed to give to his master. I often wished on these chilly mornings that I could have the same done for me.

Before dawn the oozies in charge of our travelling elephants had been out into the jungle by the light of bamboo flares in search of their animals. Sometimes these had wandered for miles, looking for the food they liked best.

Although domesticated, our elephants in Burma lived in a semi-wild state. Having done the day's work, they were perfectly free to wander off at will and were able to mix with the wild herds. In fact, sometimes the oozie would have to re-capture his elephant from right under the trunk of an amorous wild tusker who was courting her.

One day we heard one of the oozies when releasing his elephant, chatting quietly to her. He was giving her a few sound words of advice about her boy friend in the jungle.

"Don't you go to him," he was saying, "you let him come to you—you have work to do tomorrow."

This understanding between them was most important, as the affection an elephant had for its oozie was often an even stronger tie than the chains on its forelegs which fettered it when it wandered off into the wild.

Each man, too, knew his animal by the peculiarity of its footmarks, and when within ear-shot he was made doubly sure it was near by the individual sound of its bell which he had fashioned himself with great care. He would then make himself known by calling and chatting to the animal, as though it were one of his own family; and the elephant, literally chirping with pleasure, would slowly emerge from the trees and allow himself to be caught. This chirping noise which is a sign of contentment and delight can be heard from as far as a mile away; the elephant makes it by placing his tongue against the side of his cheek and then sucking in air.

Sometimes moving camp was held up because an oozie had been unable to find his animal, but it was only on rare occasions that we had to move, leaving one behind. I remember once a flirtatious female was missing and was eventually found weeks later none the worse for her dilly-dallying.

Joseph had all his livestock in their baskets, ready for the start. At dusk the evening before, Jim and I had heard squawks and cackling, as a boy had shinned up the tree in which they were roosting to catch them. During the daytime while we were in camp, the hens and ducks had made themselves quite at home, pecking about the clearing, and the ducks had even waddled down to the stream for a swim. They were such intelligent birds that I hated to think we were only taking them with us to eat them in the end. But unfortunately as our tour was to last for several months it was a necessity. Towards the end of one of our trips there were only two ducks left, which I had got really attached to, and I absolutely refused to have them killed. But I had the greatest difficulty with Joseph as I was unable to make him understand my feeling. However, I won the day and we carried them all the way home again.

Now all was ready and we were due to start on the day's march. Aung Net stooped down to pick up Tigger, the Siamese cat, to put her in her basket, but she gave a flying leap, rushed towards the nearest tall tree, and disappeared from view.

The whole party was held up—we all called appealingly, but she just climbed a few branches higher. Jim shouted to one of the jungle Burmans to shin up after her, which he did with the greatest ease. But each time, when he was within inches of capturing her, she moved on a few branches, to the delight and laughter of everybody watching below. Our servants shouted up rude remarks of advice, and the Burman in the tree was so rocking with laughter, he could hardly go on.

One of the nicest traits in the character of the Burmese was their ability to see humour in all the small things of life and to be able to laugh at themselves.

Tigger was eventually caught, and we all moved off. Each day's march was to take us a little deeper into the jungle. So far, we had been walking on a rutted red sandy track running through not very thickly timbered scrub, but now it was beginning to get narrower, and the undergrowth and trees thicker on either side. Jim and I walked well ahead with the dogs, and the elephants lumbered along some distance behind. It was still and quiet, with few of the proverbial jungle sounds.

On these early mornings the small bushes at the side of the path were draped and festooned with enormous webs made by large, poisonous looking spiders. At this hour, they were still glistening with drops of dew, like crystal chandeliers caught by shafts of early morning sunlight.

I could not resist touching one, although Jim warned me to take care as some of these spiders were poisonous and could give a nasty nip. Unlike the ordinary English cobweb, which breaks easily, I was amazed how tough it was. I could shake the drops of water from it without its coming to bits.

The path crossed and recrossed the stream bed. We were passing over it at one spot when Jim pointed out tracks in the sand made by animals that had lately been down to drink. We must have startled a leopard with our chatter, and its wet pug marks could still be seen on the rock near us. But this did not worry us, for wild animals during the daytime, if left un-molested in their natural surroundings, were not the most dangerous things in the jungle.

It was the less obvious things that were the most to be dreaded —the fevers brought on by the bite of the anopheline mosquito, the leeches, and the myriads of other pests in the rains.

In fact, Jim told me that he had felt cold with fear sometimes in heavy jungle when leeches came—not in their dozens or hundreds but in their thousands. Silently hummocking over the leaves, they crawled on, attracted by the scent of warm blood, then sank their teeth into the flesh of their victim. There they would feed, bloating themselves until they were twenty times their usual size—so fast would they cling that the only way to get them off was to touch them with a lighted cigarette end.

Dogs, too, being low on the ground, were particularly vulner-able. When a leech fastened itself inside a dog's nose, the only possible way to draw it down was to chain the dog up for several hours with a bowl of water just out of reach. As for an elephant's trunk, when they got inside that the discomfort must have been awful. Jim once found a wild tusker that had just died. It was still warm when he came across it, and as he watched, forty buffalo leeches crawled out of its trunk.

One often wondered how the wild beasts of the forest managed to exist in the rains, attacked as they were on every side by pests and parasites.

Jim and I sat down on a rock for a while to rest. He amused himself by blowing on a piece of grass between his thumbs, making a sort of screeching noise.

"If we sit quietly," he explained, "we may get an answer from a barking deer, as the sound is very like the call it makes to its mate." He did this patiently, but with no result.

Later in the day, when we were rather deeper in the jungle, we tried the same thing again, and I was thrilled to hear an answering call, quite near at hand. We sat stock still and waited and were rewarded by hearing a rustle in the undergrowth, and then by seeing the little red head of this graceful miniature deer, less than two feet high, with enormous brown soulful eyes looking at us. The next second, something frightened it and it flashed back out of sight.

Who would imagine that this delicate creature would be quite capable, with one snap of its needle-sharp canine fangs, of penetrating the skin and reaching the vital parts of a tiger or a panther?

Earlier, Jim and I had been talking of the wonderful instinct that animals have, seeming to know what is going to happen in the future. He told me how the barking deer gives this call when a rise is due in the river near its haunts.

He had noticed over and over again that when the call had been given it was suddenly as if a fleeing *corps de ballet* came dancing across the river bed and into the thicket on the other side. The turbulent flood waters would then come rushing down with massive force, but the harem of the barking deer would have been called across to safety in time. In the same way, the turtle who lays its eggs in the sand at the water's edge, seems to know how high the flood waters will rise and chooses a spot just out of danger.

The extraordinary innate instincts of animals were a great help to men working in the jungle when they had to make decisions about floating the logs and had to judge how high the water would rise. Many times Jim has pointed out to me an old nest of the weaver bird hanging from a branch above the stream bed; as usual, the bird had somehow known that her nest would be just out of reach of the floods when they came.

Our next camping site lay on the far side of a small village, and we knew we were nearing it when we saw the sunlight ahead of us filtering through the trees where the clearing had been made.

The jungle villages were nearly always surrounded by open land which had been cleared to grow the rice on which the villagers were utterly dependent. With this, and the few chickens and pigs which every family kept, each village was a contented and almost entirely self-sufficient little world with no obvious poverty.

About a dozen thatched houses were neatly arranged in the middle of the clearing, with fruit and toddy palm trees planted round about to give food and shade; it was all enclosed by a rough fence. The houses were built on stilts about eight to ten feet from the ground, with thatched roofs and walls of bamboo matting. The stairway to each one was a roughly made rickety ladder, also of bamboo—in fact, in these places bamboo was put to a hundred different uses, such as baskets, vessels for drinking, and even cradles for the babies. Near a cluster of toddy palm trees was a pagoda, dazzlingly white in the brilliant sunshine.

As we came up to the fence, a crowd of mangy reddy-brown pariah dogs rushed towards us, yapping and snarling. Molly made no move to go after them, but her hair rose on her back in disapproval. Immediately they saw her, the village dogs, always rather cowardly, rushed back under their huts.

Hearing the hullabaloo, the village headman came out to greet us. He was dressed in a neat dark blue cotton coat with frogged buttons, his gaily coloured long skirt matching the silk scarf wound round his head. Everything looked well pressed and clean. It always surprised me how spruce these village Burmans managed to look on special occasions, even in these surroundings.

As we walked through the village, I noticed a group of women sitting in a circle under a shady koko tree, having a good gossip; a scene one might see in any village anywhere in the world. Like all Burmese, they exuded friendliness and were laughing and smiling together, welcoming us as we walked towards them.

I stopped to admire one adorable naked brown-skinned baby being suckled, I thought, by his mother—but I discovered that their friendliness even included suckling each other's babies, and the child I was admiring belonged to a mother on the other side of the circle.

Its actual mother had in her arms a dark brown furry object which puzzled me. I went nearer to look, and could hardly believe my eyes—she was suckling a baby bear. I had known before that the Burmese women will suckle any young animal that has lost its mother, as part of their religious belief in the sanctity of life, but it took me completely by surprise to see it actually happening. It was strange and touching—but somehow seemed completely natural.

To one side of the village was the monastery—this was always the most important building in every jungle village. A few monks, dressed in saffron-yellow robes, lived and meditated here; but the place was also a hive of activity, and the centre of the people's lives.

Every Burmese boy must spend some time in a monastery where he is taught to read and write, and learns the ancient rites of good will and hospitality to mankind. It brought to these remote places in Burma a literacy and charitable discipline seldom found in other eastern countries.

We could hear chanting coming from the schoolroom where the children were being taught, the sound sometimes rising to a shouting pandemonium. They seemed to be yelling at the tops of their voices, but nobody minded, the idea being that if the noise stopped, the work stopped too. Even in the evenings the monastery was never silent, for the sound of the gongs summoning the monks to prayer came over the warm air and later on, when darkness fell, the tinkle of the pagoda bells would rise and fall on the night breezes.

We wandered on down the rutty track which was the main street, pigs and chickens squawking and squealing as they scuttled away from us under the houses.

We were just about to leave and were saying goodbye to the headman when Jim, in his usual way, asked if there was anything he could do for him. The man answered that his brother had run a spike of bamboo through his hand a few days ago, and he thought it was badly poisoned and would be glad if Jim would look at it. This was not entirely surprising, for Jim had quite a reputation as a 'medicine man'. Many of the sick from camps or nearby jungle villages came to him for advice.

The hand was in a dreadful state, greeny grey and stinking, almost gangrenous, and quite impossible to treat there on the spot. Jim told the headman that his brother would have to follow on with us for a few days so that he could be treated, and unless he did so he would probably lose his hand and arm. He readily agreed to this, as he was in great pain.

As soon as we arrived in camp, Jim sent for him and called for Aung Net to bring out his medicine box—this was an issue from the teak firm, containing all the elementary medicines which might be needed for the treatment of jungle ills: quinine for fevers, and various ointments, pills and bandages.

Jim then poured some hot boiled water into a basin and added permanganate crystals; having unwrapped the injured hand, he told the man to sit and soak it, giving instructions that he must come every hour while we were there and give it further soakings in front of our tent.

The man came with us for a week, and it was quite extraordinary how the injury responded to this simple treatment. Had he been a European, this would certainly have been a case for amputation, but the jungle Burman puts all his faith in a man he trusts and this, added to his native toughness, often results in what seem to be almost miraculous cures.

Chapter XII

ELEPHANTS AT WORK

O N leaving the village we set off crossing the paddy fields. They had already been reaped and were looking almost like English cornfields, covered in golden stubble. But we had to leave this sunlit world behind us as we stepped back under the huge trees into the forest again. The dusty bullock tracks which up to now we had been walking on gradually petered out till they were no more than narrow ways made by big game. Just as cows in a field always seem to tread the same paths, so do wild animals, and it was along these jungle trails that we now made our course.

Somewhere along this route we were expecting to be met by a young Assistant, Tony Stewart, who was in charge of the area to which we were going.

We knew that he would be eagerly awaiting our arrival, as the sort of life these young men had to lead was extremely lonely. They worked out here by themselves, often several days' journey away from fellow Europeans, and I think some of the finest men I knew were these Assistants employed by the big timber firms extracting teak from the Burma jungles. The very nature of their work demanded qualities which no advertisement for such posts could ever specify.

As well as being extremely tough and self-reliant, they had to have initiative to take decisions on the spot without reference to higher authority. They had to be diplomatic, firm, and yet understanding of the native Burman. They were his master, friend and adviser, and more often than not, also his doctor and banker as well. They not only had to speak Burmese fluently, but, to do the job properly, they had to think the Burmese way.

They developed an unusual love and understanding of the animals in their care, more especially the elephants whom they recognised and treated as fellow beings. They knew their names and characters, and very important too, the characters of the men who were their oozies, sitting on their heads.

Their dogs too were an integral part of their lives, as they depended on them for company when the day's work was done.

Jim himself had been an Assistant for ten years and well knew the loneliness of the life—sometimes he had been alone for as long as eleven months on end. He told me how in the evenings he and his old bull mastiff Juno would sit at table opposite each other, and he would find himself telling the dog of all the day's doings—glad for once to have a chance to speak his own language.

Even though the fear of hydrophobia was one of the biggest curses of a jungle Assistant's life, he would never part with his dogs. One young Assistant we knew was taken to Mandalay hospital before he developed the full symptoms of this dread disease. He eventually died and the surgeon and his staff kept the cause of death a strict secret for a considerable time, and it never got to the ears of the other Assistants in the jungle. The surgeon handled many of these young men and knew what a terrible blow it would be to them and how upset they would be if any sort of rule came about forbidding them to have dogs. He knew that in any case it would never be kept.

Very often in the wet season life was almost unbearably depressing—the whole jungle became an infested swamp, a green dank hell, the silence only broken by the monotonous drip from the trees. It was then that the nerves of the weaker man would give out, even if he were able to keep physically fit, which in this humid sticky heat was almost impossible; there were constant attacks of malaria to put up with, and running sores caused by the insects in the infected mud.

One of these was the chegre or jigger, a parasite of the

minutest size which gets under the skin. It buries its eggs and expands, setting up most acute irritation often leading to ulcers. Frequently they settled under the toe-nails and finger-nails, where they were next to impossible to get at—even though in some districts there were natives who made a living by extracting them. Another was the hookworm, an almost microscopic creature thriving in damp soil, and usually entering the blood stream through the feet and ending up in the intestines. It plays havoc with the system and may even cause temporary paralysis.

It is perhaps not surprising that only three per cent of the Europeans who lived this life were able to survive twenty-five years of it.

But now it was the dry season, the weather was perfect, and after we had been trekking along for about an hour, Tony eventually appeared, striding towards us with his two dogs, and looking full of health and energy.

He came up with a wide smile, and I remember thinking how extremely good looking he was. I had not met him before, but Jim had told me about him and that he was a young man whom he thought very highly of. He was only twenty-three, but had already proved himself equal to the life and efficient in his job.

He had been on his own now for about three months, and was clearly delighted that he was now going to have our company for a few days.

That evening, we all sat and chatted together. Tony, to regale us, had obviously saved up his best food and drink and we had quite a party. Jim pulled his leg and enjoyed taking him out of himself and making him laugh.

Tony told us how the background of his life had changed from one extreme to another. He had previously been in the navy, where there had been no privacy at all and sometimes he had longed for it, and now here he was in this job where there was nothing else. He was a little anxious, he said, whether the girl whom he was engaged to at home would find it altogether too lonely out here when they were married, as being an Assistant's wife, she would have months in the station by herself while he was away in the jungle. He was hoping at any rate they would get a good posting. It was rather touching the way he kept bringing the conversation back to this girl, and I felt sure that it gave him comfort and that she was somehow brought nearer to him when he was talking about her.

"Would you believe it," said Jim at breakfast next morning, "I have got yet another patient to deal with. One of Tony's elephants had an accident yesterday—a log fell onto its fore-foot, injuring the toenail badly. Would you like to come up to the logging camp with us, to see it?"

I had very much been looking forward to going up and watching the elephants dragging in any case, so was eager to go with them now.

We climbed through dense jungle to the top of the ridge, and then down the other side, Jim and Tony inspecting teak stumps on the way. Here, in a clearing in the jungle, was the elephant camp where the elephants were brought in and saddled for their logging work. It consisted of a collection of bamboo huts, some for the oozies to live in, and a small one for stores and provisions, while another little shack housed the elephants' medicines. To one side was a huge, crudely made, saddle rack, and it was here that the elephants were harnessed with their jungle-made gear before going off to work.

Tied up near the saddle rack was the injured elephant. Its oozie untethered him and made him go down in the hmit or sitting position, with his forelegs straight out in front of him.

Jim walked over to have a look at him, and though rumbling and obviously nervous, the animal made no fuss as he bent over to examine the injured foot. The nail was crushed, and it looked a pulpy mess. I was astonished once more at the atmosphere of mutual confidence shown between Jim and his animal patient.

Talking soothingly in Burmese all the time he first cut away part of the putrid flesh, and then applied a dressing of Stockholm tar. It must have been an excruciatingly painful operation, but the elephant never moved.

Jim told Tony to have the animal sent away to a rest camp, and we heard later that although the nail never grew again the skin where it had been became calloused and hard as horn, and that the foot was in full use again.

Having treated the elephant, we pushed on through the jungle to see the timber work.

The logging camp was on the bank of a stream and the great logs were being laid out by the elephants ready for launching into the torrents when the first rises came flooding down, later on in the year. Small timber poles, rather like pit props, lay across the track acting as crude rollers to help with the dragging.

There is no animal to equal the elephant in strength, or with the power to work and live in the jungle. His amazing trunk is capable of lifting a log weighing a ton, and yet has the precision to pick up a pin. He can drag huge tree trunks of anything up to five or six tons across most difficult jungle tracks, and then guide them with perfect judgment to the edge of a ravine, where they will hurtle down to the dry river-bed below, to await the floods which will float them down, on their long journey to the saw mills, taking possibly several years to do so.

An elephant had to be at least twenty years of age before he was capable of doing this heavy work, and in the old days the teak companies never thought it worth while to breed elephants in captivity and then have to look after them for twenty years before they were useful, so they bought wild adult elephants instead. These had been captured by natives who drove them into large enclosures called 'kheddars' where they were left in the full heat of the blazing sun without food or water until they were broken in heart and spirit. They lost condition rapidly, and in their desperation finally gave in and did what was required of them.

This terrible cruelty was still in practice when Jim first went to Burma and was one of the things he passionately fought against. He had always felt that calves born in domesticity were an asset that had been very much wasted, especially as elephants brought up from birth in the camps were much healthier and more reliable than those caught from the wild. They did not cost much to feed either, as they were allowed to wander off and forage for themselves, and the only expense involved was the oozies' wages. Jim and others eventually persuaded the authorities to see the sense of this, and later on their working herds were entirely built up from calves born and reared in captivity.

The calf was broken in at the age of about five, a young oozie being chosen for it at the same time. He and the elephant grew up so closely together and with such trust in each other that a remarkable relationship was formed. This could never have been brought about had a wild animal been rather brutally broken in when it was already adult, and then handled by a strange oozie. As it was, the two young things understood each other perfectly.

The calf elephant, too, often behaves rather like a child, with its adventurous spirit, naughtiness and disobedience. Some of the elephants here in this camp had their calves with them, and we saw one youngster wander away out of sight of its mother because he had found something good to eat. Quite obviously he could hear her anxious call because he listened with one ear cocked, and stopped chewing for a minute, but he chose to pretend he could not hear, and went on stuffing his mouth again.

After about half an hour, his mother started calling in earnest, and much more sternly. He seemed to know that now the moment had come when he had to give in, and he rushed back to her through the undergrowth. Just like a human mother, she gave him a tremendous ticking-off, and a hard slap with her trunk on his tummy, which sounded like a drum—as much as to say "That will teach you!" It completely winded the poor little thing, but after that he was a picture of abject obedience.

Some of the elephants were dragging singly, others in pairs, but what amused me most were the mother elephants with calves at heel. The calves walked head to head with their mothers, trying to pretend that they were dragging too. When the going was extra hard and the mother elephant had to lunge and urge with all her strength to force the log along, the small calf would do the same with its imaginary log. The noise and fuss it made must have worn it out.

One would have imagined that when the calf started his training at five or six years old there would have been great pining when he and his mother had to be parted, but there was no display of grief, although a great affection always remained between them, and they would always recognise each other immediately even after quite a number of years had elapsed.

Once when Jim came to inspect a camp, an eighteen-year-old calf which was one of his travelling transport, saw its mother and they both at once chirped with delight, and later, when they were turned loose to feed in the jungle, they joined up together. This happened every evening while he was in that area; however, they did not seem to mind when the time came for parting.

On the other hand, it is always a pathetic thing if a very young calf is left an orphan through its mother dying for some reason. Few of these baby elephants live very long alone, as they are unable to feed themselves.

A touching thing once happened when one of Jim's elephants died, leaving a female calf. A large male tusker tried to look after it and adopt it. It was pitiable to see the calf hunting round for the udders which were not there, and how this huge male elephant with all its good will could not help the youngster. With a lot of patience and care Jim and the oozies were

The young oozie with his baby elephant

Climbing up a ridge to reach a log

Travelling elephant being unloaded

eventually able to wean it on to bamboo shoots, and all was well.

On another occasion, Jim gave permission for two Burmese women to suckle an orphan calf. An elephant's udders are smaller than the human breast, and the elephant calf is so delicate and gentle in the way it takes the milk that it does not hurt its foster mother.

Further on up the valley we came across a real spot of trouble. Some logs had been launched when a spate was on, but had failed to get away, and were now piled in a mountainous mass high and dry on the boulders. It was extraordinary that they had not been smashed to pulp. In fact they often did get just such a battering, and finished up so banged about and frayed that they looked just like gigantic shaving brushes, and were useless as timber.

I was amazed to see the agility of the large elephants working on this pile. They almost looked as if they were playing a very earnest game of spillikins, so cleverly did they select the key log and then very gently rock it to and fro with a forefoot until the exact minute when they knew the whole thing would start to move. Then, stepping adroitly out of harm's way, they stood aside and watched the immense pile come crashing down. The oozie on the elephant's head left all judgment in this delicate job to his animal, who knew better than he did just the right moment to make the move.

The rider and his animal have a long day together, starting before dawn and often having to go many miles up and down, through dense and precipitous jungle country, till they reach the log which either has to be pushed or pulled until it is accessible to a floating stream. They work together until about three o'clock in the afternoon; then return to camp, where the elephant is unharnessed, fettered, and allowed to wander off to look for food.

The oozie then settles down to repair damaged harness and to see that all is in order for the next day's work. His toil

G

97

seems never done, but he is always smiling and cheerful, his great fondness for his elephant contributing to his contentment in life, for he is really closer to him than he is to many of his own family and will probably have spent more time with him, having lived and worked with the same animal from about the age of fourteen to forty.

Chapter XIII

THE JUNGLE STRIKES

Tony was going to accompany us for the next week while we toured his area; he and Jim had a great deal of office work to do as well as timber to inspect.

It was the custom, when meeting up with another forest man, for us all to feed together, the two cooks providing the meals on alternate days. This gave each set of servants a rest day, which they welcomed and deserved.

Our present camp site was on the banks of an almost dried up river-bed—a flat patch of brown silty sand interspersed with a coarse green grass. It was hot, dry and dusty at mid-day, as we were just beyond the shade of the forest trees, but surprisingly cold at night when the breeze came blowing down the stream bed.

I remember sitting by the fire the second evening, muffled in heavy sweaters, watching the fountains of sparks as they were blown by the cool night wind into the darkness. Even near the fire it was chilly.

I had been looking forward to another gay evening with Jim and Tony. It was our turn to do the cooking, and I had tried to think up a meal which I hoped would be something different from those that Tony usually gave himself.

Throughout the evening, though, I had a feeling that he was not in anything like the good spirits he had been in the night before, and was a bit worried when, quite early on, he asked us if we would mind if he turned in as he thought he must have caught a chill.

99

"I hope to goodness it is only a chill," Jim said. "I can't imagine him giving up this evening unless he feels really rotten."

However, we did not think much more about it, and we all went to bed.

We had planned to move on next morning; but when Aung Net came to call us, he said that Tony was down with a bout of fever. This was quite a usual occurrence in the jungle, and didn't worry Jim overmuch—he sent a message to say he would be over to see him as soon as he was dressed.

But Tony had a high temperature, and all the symptoms of a severe attack of malaria. "We certainly shan't be able to move on to-day," said Jim, "but bad as he is now, the whole thing may easily pass in another twenty-four hours."

By evening we knew we were wrong. None of the treatment for malaria had any effect at all, and I was disturbed to see that Jim was beginning to get really worried. Tony's temperature had gone up to nearly 105°, and he was now delirious at times.

We took it in turns to be with him in his tent throughout that night. As I sat on a little cane stool by the side of his bed, and looked at his deathly pale face by the light of the hurricane lamp, an awful feeling of helplessness came over me. Only the day before I had been admiring his strong good looks and obvious fitness, and now suddenly all energy seemed to have been drained from him. His blue eyes were glazed and staring —he had changed alarmingly.

It had always given me a feeling of great confidence, that Jim, having lived so long in the jungle, would be able to cope with most of the illnesses that were likely to occur. If he could not help now, who could? I reckoned it would take at least three days going all out, to get Tony to medical aid, and I couldn't imagine it would be possible to move him in any case. However, we both determined not to let either see the other's anxiety.

After what seemed a very long night, dawn began to break and the oil lamp was finally put out. I felt greatly relieved when, at this moment, Jim appeared in the doorway of the tent. I could see, merely by looking at him, that he had come to a decision.

"I don't know what is wrong with him," he said—"all I do know is that this chap must be got to hospital—we'll pack up now and beat it for the railway."

This was easier said than done—the railway was over thirty miles away, and about five days' normal marching through some of the most difficult hill country in Burma. I could not help being horrified at the thought of what this journey might do to the patient, but we had no choice—it had to be done.

Knowing the urgency, the Burmans hurried all they could to get the camp ready to move off. Jim got two of them to make a sort of improvised stretcher by slinging a long camp chair between two poles, and we wrapped Tony up in blankets and laid him on it.

Our aim was to try to reach a village ten miles on before the midday heat. Here Jim hoped to be able to hire a bullock cart for the rest of the journey.

We walked in single file, followed by the elephants, four oozies carrying the stretcher ahead of us. They did everything they could to hold it level, but the unevenness of the ground made it quite impossible to keep it straight and avoid jolting.

Apart from his fever, Tony had to put up with the awful discomfort of this journey for seven hours, and there was little we could do for him. He was conscious for a great part of the time, but never once complained. We were all dead beat, but extremely relieved, when towards midday we came in sight of the village and were able to set up camp in the shade nearby.

Camped under the trees that evening, we did all we could to make him comfortable, but the long trek had taken it out of him. He spoke in a sort of delirium of home and his girl and happier days. Perhaps it was well that his wandering thoughts could bridge the gap that lay between.

Next morning the bullock cart arrived. These carts give a

very rocky ride at the best of times, with their solid wooden uneven and creaking wheels, and I really dreaded the next twenty-three miles for Tony.

To try to make things a little easier for him, Jim had a platform of plaited bamboo made and fitted it above the wooden floor of the cart. This did seem to help on level ground, but when we came to anything of a slope, it tended to be too slippery, as poor Tony was unable to hang on or help himself in any way.

Except for an occasional halt to give him some water and have some ourselves, we travelled all day. There was no real road, just a rutty track, up one deep densely wooded hillside and down the next, and through dried-up stream beds axle-deep in soft sand. These the bullocks were quite unable to take at a gentle pace, and in order to get up the steep bank on the further side of the ravine, the driver had to make them take the downward slope at a gallop, hoping the impetus would carry them up the other side. It was torture, and Jim decided the only thing to do was to lie beside Tony on the cart, with his arm round him, trying to spare him the worst of the racketing.

Ten hours later, I was walking like an automaton in a kind of daze, too tired to feel much any more; but I do remember the thankfulness when we came out into the open and saw the wayside station and knew that this nightmare journey was nearly over and that Tony would soon be in the train on his way to hospital. It was pathetic to see the look of relief which crossed his face when he felt the firmness of the railway carriage seat beneath his aching body.

After we had been in the train all day and were just crossing over the Ava bridge, our journey to Mandalay was nearly at an end. It was one of those evenings with a superb sunset and unbelievable colours that one only gets in the East. Tony was for the first time a little conscious of his surroundings. Putting his arm round his shoulders to support him, Jim lifted the carriage blind.

"You must look at this, old man," he said. "It's wonderful."

Tony, gazing down over the Irrawaddy River, turned to Jim, smiling for the first time. "Billy, you're the best doctor a man ever had—how did you know what seeing that would do for me?"

We had almost a feeling of triumph when Tony was safely installed in hospital. The thought that he would finally get the treatment he needed had kept us going on this journey, and somehow I do not think we had allowed ourselves to feel that it could all be in vain.

From the charts of the fever that Jim had kept so carefully since the beginning, the doctor was able to diagnose enteric— a dangerous, but not incurable, illness. He said he thought that, being young, there was every chance they would be able to pull him through.

But, alas, Tony was not to live; pneumonia unexpectedly developed, and three days later he died. We both felt heartbroken and that somehow we had failed this courageous young man, and I don't think in all our married life I have ever seen Jim so deeply moved and depressed as when we started on our journey back together.

Chapter XIV

THE RULE OF THE *NATS*

THERE were signs everywhere of the approaching hot weather, and after we had been on tour for just over three months, we headed back towards Mawlaik. We had had a grilling day's march in open dusty country—dry winds rustled the almost leafless trees and everything seemed to be slowly scorching up. This is the time of year when the sap of the deciduous trees rests and when all the fauna seem to disappear and hibernate. We were beginning to feel sucked dry ourselves, and were longing to reach the next halt.

Jim had planned to camp by the side of a perennial stream—now only a trickle, but the thought of it babbling over the pebbles was cooling in itself. He thought he remembered that there was a large shady evergreen nyaung tree in this place. How glad we were to find he was right; we both sighed with relief as we sat in its shade, sheltering from the fierce heat.

Molly took this opportunity to cool herself off by lying belly deep in the middle of the stream bed. I longed to follow her example, but contented myself with dangling my feet in the water.

When the elephants arrived, Jim gave orders for our tent to be pitched under the tree; but a few moments later, Aung Net came running up in a great state of agitation. He told us that the oozies were most reluctant to put our tent here, as the tree was inhabited by a *nat sin*—the spirit of a wild elephant—and should we insist on doing so, we would be risking dire calamity.

"Blast!" said Jim. "It's the only shade for miles round."

We were both tempted to ignore their warnings. However, it was the season of sudden thunderstorms and a nyaung tree is apt to crash with very little warning. We knew, too, that if anything did happen they would immediately say it was because we had flaunted the *nats*. We were both rather superstitious, anyway, but I must say we cursed that *nat* when we had to sweat it out under hot canvas in the midday sun.

As other countries have their fairies, pixies and gnomes, so do the Burmese have their *nats*. And although Buddhism has been established in Burma since 240 B.C. and is deeply believed in, the *nats*, or spirits of nature, are the remnants of an older belief and they still have a great hold on the minds of the people. In fact, with the lower-class Burman, the *nat* worship, or revering of the spirits, sometimes comes before his religion. The *nat* is destructive and needs propitiating every day, whereas worship at the pagodas is only a weekly duty. Near every village there is a little shrine built for him, and here morsels of food, pots of water, and sometimes flowers, are placed every day.

There is always the guardian *nat* of the home and to please him the posts in the houses are covered with a hood of white cloth, for it is here he takes up his abode. Special water is put out for him and is sprinkled about the house as a protection. In spite of all these offerings, the *nat* has little regard for the householders, and it is only to allay his anger and to prevent him from doing them awful injury that he must be appeased by these gifts.

If a member of the family should be dying, the local monk is usually called in, but with no idea of giving spiritual comfort or extreme unction. In the Buddhist religion, no last-minute repentances can change the balance of merit and demerit which has accumulated over a lifetime. It is merely that his good influence and the piety of his calling are supposed to keep away the vindictive *nats*.

Whenever Jim started on some project in the forest the jungle Burmans always had to build a little thatched shrine on stilts for the *nats* before starting work. Even the path leading up to such a shrine is treated with great reverence, and Jim warned me if ever we came on one in the jungle to try to avoid walking on it. After living among the Burmese for nearly ten years, he had come to have a great respect for their beliefs, and even for their stuperstitions. He told me an amusing story of how, when he first came out to Burma, he was put properly in his place about these things by a tough old Forest Manager who took them very seriously.

It was during his first day's march in the jungle that he noticed a pile of stones like a cairn at the base of a large tree. He asked the Forest Manager what it was.

"Goodness knows when," was the reply, "but probably centuries ago, there was an elephant camp here under this nyaung tree which, being an evergreen, is said by the Burmans to give out a ton of evaporated water a day. Ever since then, a *nat* or spirit is believed to have lived here; and everyone who passes by respects it by placing something at the base of the tree as an offering. Often the Burman has nothing to give, so he just puts on a stone as he goes by—hence this pile here. I myself shall place a cheroot on it—you can put anything you like, your shirt for all I care, but put something you must, and don't talk while you're doing it."

They moved on, the Forest Manager placing his cigar on the pile as he passed. Jim, following closely behind, light-heartedly tossed his handkerchief on top of the cheroot. The forest manager, seeing him smiling, turned on him angrily, saying, "Are you trying to be funny?"

"Well," said Jim, "I expect the old *nat* gets a cold in the head sometimes and needs a handkerchief—how do you know he smokes, anyway?"

The Forest Manager was obviously furious. "You'll learn not to joke about such things in time," he said.

It was not until that moment that it dawned on Jim that this old Jungle Salt was completely in earnest, and he was amazed at his naïveté. But he was a west-countryman and rather superstitious himself—also, he always had an innate respect for the feelings of others, and in years to come, I have heard him mildly rebuking his juniors for laughing at native superstitions.

"Never laugh at things you don't understand," he would say, "there may be much more in them than you know. At any rate, you will be safer to treat them seriously while you are in the jungle, as so many of them spring from a practical foundation. In any case, a lot of us have strange convictions, but if they help us, why destroy them?"

One day I remember talking to a timber contractor who was faced with the difficult job of getting a very large log of teak out of the most inaccessible place. He and his men and their team of buffaloes had left their village long before daylight to set about hauling it to the river bank, but it had got stuck.

It was hours later that Jim and I came upon them—the log was covered for its entire length with small dishes of rice, plantains, eggs, bamboo shoots, and other delicacies. The contractor and all his men were squatting on the ground in contemplation—they were appeasing the *nats*, somewhat on the principle of paying an insurance premium. The contractor grinned impishly as he explained what they were doing—Jim and I felt we must wait and see the results.

Considerably later the team of buffaloes was harnessed up once more, to try to drag the log out. There wasn't a hitch, and as they pulled it away, the contractor looked round with a self-satisfied smile as if to say, I told you so!

Now the elephants too were beginning to feel the heat. They do not like the hot sun and in their natural state live a nocturnal life, as do most animals in the jungle. We would watch them trying to keep themselves cool by placing their trunks down their throats and sucking up water, which they were able to retain in their stomachs, then squirting it over themselves.

The timber companies took great care of their animals. Most of the jobs they did were carried out in the shade of the forest, and they were seldom, if ever, tethered, and certainly never in the sun.

I remember we once saw an unfortunate elephant working in a native timber yard—it had been tied up in the heat, with no shade, and was desperately trying to cover its head by throwing up trunkfuls of hay, sacks, and anything else that was within reach, in a vain attempt to protect itself from the burning heat.

It was no wonder that our elephants were beginning to get irritable. Apart from the heat, they found that many of the trees were leafless when they wandered off to look for their food, and the six hundred pounds of fodder each of them needed daily to keep its digestion in order took some finding.

Wisps of hot air stirred the large leaves on the ground, and the wild animals had moved away deeper into the forest to places where they knew they could find something to eat and drink. But the elephants' turn was coming. Directly this tour was over, their oozies would be taking them for a holiday for the whole of the six weeks of the hot weather—to one of the special rest camps deep in the heart of evergreen jungle. These camps were situated by the side of the larger, continuously flowing rivers, and were provided for all elephants working in the jungle. Without these periods of rest in very hot weather, the beasts would be unable to stand up to the arduous work they had to undertake in the following rains.

The oozie would take his family with him to the camp and both he and the elephant got a well-deserved rest. The elephant is, in fact, one of the family, and I remember once, when visiting a rest camp with Jim, seeing an elephant baby-sitting for them. The oozie had put his baby girl to play on the ground, and had drawn a large circle in the sand all round her; he then gave orders to the elephant not to allow her to crawl outside this improvised playpen. The baby, of course, immediately did so, but every time she attempted to escape, the elephant gently but firmly lifted her back again. The family went about their business with perfect confidence in their nursemaid.

There was no period of rest, however, for the Forest Assistant. In both wet and dry seasons his life was a busy and a hard one. Now, when the logs were stuck hard and fast in the hot dried-up trails of sand that had once been streams, he had to take the opportunity to count the numbers and tonnage; a really gruelling job, as he worked in the full sun amongst the stranded timber shimmering in the heat.

I can remember Jim telling me that in the days when he had to do this job, the heat from the sand would penetrate the soles of his boots until it felt as though he were walking on fire. The reflection of the blinding sunshine, both from the sand and the logs, brought on such eye strain that in spite of dark glasses he would finish up each day with a tearing headache. Now that he was a Forest Manager, he was at least reprieved from this particular job.

He was at this moment, however, beginning to get restive, like the elephants. We had been without mail for a week and cigarettes had run out, added to which for some days past he had had a toothache which was nagging at him most of the time—not a good moment for the elephants to stampede, but that is exactly what they did.

We were loading up in the early morning before the day's march when the tarpaulins covering a pile of tins stacked on the back of Po Sin, Joseph's "kitchen" elephant, slipped off, bringing the whole lot clanging to the ground.

Po Sin was already on edge with the heat, and this was too much for him and he was thoroughly startled. Curling up his trunk like a watch spring, as elephants always do in times of danger, and closing his little piggy eyes—he charged.

His oozie, taken unawares, was flung off as his animal ploughed through the waiting group of travellers, and away into the jungle beyond. He tore through the thick clumps of bamboo and undergrowth, scattering the remains of his load as he went, and frightening himself even more with the noise.

The other nineteen elephants, who had been patiently standing waiting and ready to start, were terrified, and to our horror they suddenly swung themselves round, stuck their tails straight out behind them, and went stampeding off after him.

Luckily their oozies hung on for all they were worth. Shouting with one accord to their animals "Yat like sin, Yat like sin" (Stop elephant, stop), they were eventually able to control them and bring them back to camp.

As for Po Sin, he had disappeared into the thick of the forest with his oozie in hot pursuit; and Jim gave orders to move on without them.

It was not until three days after that the oozie caught up with us and came shamefacedly to Jim, saying, "He's lost, Thakin, he's lost." Jim was none too pleased, as each one of our elephants was worth from three to five thousand pounds.

"Go back and search until you find him, however long it takes," he said.

It did take a long time—it was not until three months later, when we were back in Mawlaik, that we heard that Po Sin had been recaptured, minus all his harness, feeding happily amongst a herd of wild elephants. In spite of his long spell of freedom, he chirruped with delight when he saw his oozie again, and was quite willing to go with him.

Chapter XV

THE DOC

SHORTLY after our return to Mawlaik, Jim's tooth really began to play up. There was no dentist within hundreds of miles, and he had been hoping very much that it might right itself.

"It's no good," he said one evening, "the coming out can't be worse than it is at the moment, and I couldn't possibly tour in the rains until it has gone. I shall have to go to Dr. Algy Bell."

He called himself Dr. Algy Bell. By all appearances he was an Indian and where he inherited his name from I would not dare to guess. He was what was known in those days as a Sub-Assistant Surgeon: one of a band of men constituting a Service—some of whom claimed medical experience and knowledge equal to all the specialists in hospitals of tropical medicine or famous streets.

In the past, Jim had more than once had to place not only his own life, but those of young fellow Assistants in his hands.

The Doc was a simple man with a heart of gold. His hospital, in this small up-country riverine station, was merely a bamboo hut with matting walls; an apology for a hospital. He never grumbled, but revelled in the thought of being a pioneer.

His district covered many thousands of square miles of forests and villages. He rarely went on tour, but he had won the confidence of villagers living in the most outlandish spots.

Jim had known him from the very early days. He used to come back from the jungle having had to deal with illnesses and accidents, and was glad to discuss them with the doctor. These were not only amongst his elephant riders, their wives and families, but there were what appeared to him then as insurmountable troubles, both medical and surgical, with his elephants.

Nevertheless it was difficult to persuade his human patients to go to the Doc, and most of them had to be treated in the elephant camp. Only in cases of real emergency, such as serious accidents, could he make them go to the little hospital.

As far as he could remember, it was malaria that first brought them together—for one thing Jim was riddled with it himself. In the jungle a go of malaria was thought no more of than a cold in the head. "Treble up quinine for a week and for God's sake don't catch a chill on it," was the advice the Doc would give. For it was pneumonia on top of malaria which could be fatal.

Jim learnt a lot about malaria from him. The Doc made him up big bottles of concentrated liquid quinine—laced with arsenic as a tonic. Huge doses up to thirty grains a day were prescribed. When Jim gave this to the oozies their heads must have sung, but it kept the disease under control.

This was not all. It was the encouragement of his doctor friend that taught Jim, young and inexperienced as he was, to have no qualms where medical attention was needed.

It so happened that soon after Jim started work in the jungle he had to face an emergency resulting in the most shocking wounds he had ever seen. A honey bear had scalped one of his tree fellers. By the time Jim saw him, his scalp was falling over his face, the long black hair still hanging from it and matted with dried blood. Jim soaked the hair in warm water and then after cutting it off, folded the scalp back on the top of the head. This was horrifying enough, but when he exposed his face, Jim found that one eye had been taken from its socket. It was damaged but he managed to get it back under what was left of the lid. Worse still were the man's upper and lower lips. The bear's centre claw had exposed the jaw bone. In a way

What a height to climb for a tit-bit!

Baby elephant
seeking shade
under its mother

Bath time

this was a mercy, for if it had not got the jaw, his Adam's apple would have been taken right out, and Jim would not have known how to deal with that. The attempt to hold the hare lip together was almost as much agony to Jim as to the unfortunate tree feller. Finally he got an ordinary large-size needle and thread through the skin and tied a knot, probably a granny at that. He had patched up the poor man as best he could, and three days later was able to put him in the hands of the Doc.

A month afterwards Jim saw the Doc and the patient. The man was alive and recovering—it seemed like a miracle. The Doc congratulated him, adding: "Your stitching was not all that good—you had better come and watch me operate. I think I will also give you a proper needle and some surgical thread to carry in your first-aid box."

The following day Jim attended an operation. He told me that to describe the 'theatre' would be more gruesome than the operation itself. The patient was a young Burmese woman. She was already under the anaesthetic, lying on a table so narrow that he felt that if she sighed she would roll off. But she was unconscious. A young Burmese nurse, the Doc and Jim were the only people present, and completely filled the little space there was in the dismal room.

The nurse then turned back an apology for a sterilized sheet, exposing one breast. "She's got yaws," said the doctor. "The other has gone, but there's nothing else for it—I shall have to remove this one too." Yaws was a contagious disease amongst the natives, causing bright red swellings. Jim shuddered as he watched him working, and he told me that all he could remember was a bottle of iodine being douched on by the little nurse. He said he thought he must have closed his eyes and not opened them again until he heard the Doc saying, "Now look here." He looked—the breast had gone. All he could see were the incision marks where the skin had been folded flat back covering the place where the curve had been.

* * *

Nowadays whenever Jim and I met Dr. Algy Bell, which was frequently, he always had some story to tell and it was no exception this time. Having finished a long description of a case he had been dealing with, he turned his attention to the matter in hand—Jim's tooth. He said quite frankly that he had no cocaine or pain deadener to inject but promised Jim instant relief once it was extracted, if he could stick it, and he advised him to have a couple of stiff pegs of whisky before coming to have it out.

That evening, with Molly at our heels, we set off. At the hospital, the Doc put Jim to sit in a good solid chair with wooden arms, which he told him to grip tightly. This Jim did, determined to take the chair with him should necessity arise. I noted what a short stocky little man the doctor was as he went towards him.

His only preliminary was to swab the gums with tincture of iodine. "Shout if you want to," he said. "It would only be natural as you've had no pain killer."

He got hold of the tooth, and I saw Jim flinch with pain—it must have been hell. When he could stick it in silence no longer, he gave a groan—but there was worse to come, both for him and for the doctor.

At this moment Molly, who had been lying in a corner of the room and whom we had completely forgotten, took a flying leap at Doctor Bell and got as firm a grip on his buttocks as the Doc had on Jim's tooth. The little Indian yelled, but didn't let go. He seemed to lift Jim, chair and all, then something gave—the tooth was out.

The Doc and Jim faced each other, he holding the bloody tooth in his forceps, and Jim still gripping the arms of the chair. I was clinging hard to Molly, who was all tensed up and longing to have another go.

"So sorry, Doc," said Jim, to which he replied:

"Tie up that ruddy dog of yours; you'll have to treat me now—get some iodine on to my buttocks as quickly as you can."

I managed to get Molly out of the room, and left Jim to patch things up as best he could. He became the doctor, with Doctor Bell as the patient—pants down. After that, they both needed more than two stiff pegs of whisky to overcome their experiences.

"We ought never to have taken Molly with us," Jim said that evening. "We must have been mad. I might have known she would attack anybody who she thought was hurting me." But Molly was Jim's constant companion, and it had never entered either of our heads to leave her at home.

Her faithfulness was sometimes tricky. Jim always had to remember to tell her it was all right even when his own servant Aung Net, whom she knew well, was taking off his shoes.

Luckily, she was wonderfully obedient. When we were out with the elephants, Jim would usually make her sit quite a long way away, as they hated a dog running round them—I saw an elephant once lash out at an Assistant's dog which walked in front of it and break its back with one flick of its trunk.

When she and Jim were in the jungle they seemed to have a silent understanding of each other. One day he was walking with Molly at his heels as usual when, wanting to blow his nose, he felt in his breast pocket for his handkerchief—it wasn't there. Patting the empty pocket, he turned and said to me, "Damn it all, I must have dropped my hankie further back, when I pulled out my cigarettes."

Molly, without further ado, dashed back along the path where we had just come, and we couldn't think what she was after. In less than five minutes, she came trotting up, carrying the handkerchief in her mouth.

"However did she know?" I asked.

"Well, whenever I've lost something," said Jim, "I've always called Molly and then patted the empty pocket. She knows that means she must hunt around—now she is getting so darned clever, I evidently don't even have to ask her."

One thing I was always grateful to Molly for was her

magnanimity towards me. She was so possessive, and yet she never showed any signs of jealousy, accepting me from the beginning as part of Jim's life.

In spite of her docile nature and gentle tawny colouring, she could look quite alarming; and when roused or on guard the long creamy ruff round her neck would stand bristling on end as she stood stiff in every muscle.

When he went off in the morning, if for some reason Jim did not want to take her with him, he would drop his bunch of keys on the top of the large iron-bound teak box which he used for a safe, and say, "Watch this for me, Molly."

She understood perfectly, and woe betide anybody who came too near. Having a duty to perform, she forgot to feel insulted at being left behind and was quite happy until Jim returned.

In fact, he seldom went anywhere without her. She even went with him on the difficult wet-weather jungle tours, when great care had to be taken of her as they travelled through the deep mud and torrential rivers. No doubt her presence caused Jim extra anxiety, and at times it must have been very difficult going for poor Molly, but they both preferred to have it this way rather than be parted. I was glad—I always felt Jim was safer when she was with him.

CHAPTER XVI

A PREDICAMENT WITH POISON

WE stuck the hot weather out in Mawlaik. Nearly all
activity came to a standstill, and one seemed to drag
through the day alternately sweating and resting. Jim
often used to say, when he came home after a sweltering day
in the office, how much he envied the elephants refreshing
themselves in their holiday camp by the river with no work
to do.

Later in the evenings, when the sun had lost some of its fire,
he would go off to play polo, a game that he loved—although
I could never understand how anyone enjoyed anything so
vigorous in this battening heat. The ponies and the players
would come off the field in a muck sweat, and with an almost
unquenchable thirst. The Indian grooms then started wiping
their ponies down with straw, and in no time at all had them
looking clean, refreshed, and cool once more, their coats like
satin.

The nights were almost as hot as the days, and one got little
restful sleep. We did not sleep outside for fear of the heavy
night dew bringing on fever, and would wander from room
to room and bed to bed trying to keep cool, but each one
seemed only hotter than the last. We used no bedding—just
rice mats spread on the webbing—and it was nothing out of
the ordinary for me to wake up in one part of the house and
Jim in another.

Ever since I had been out here, I had heard people talking
about the horrors of Burma in the wet season; but now, in
spite of the fact that we still managed to get a lot of enjoyment

out of life, I could not help longing for the rains to break. The hot winds blowing ceaselessly had a stultifying effect on one's mind and body.

It was a strict rule with the Bombay Burmah Corporation that no wives were allowed to tour in the forests in the rainy season. The jungle tracks were deep in mud—infectious and breeding disease—and the rivers were flooding and dangerous, quite apart from the multitudes of pests which come to life in the dampness and humidity. It was no place for a woman. In any case, the men had enough on their shoulders without that responsibility. It was during the monsoons that work in the forest was at its highest pitch. All the timber was waiting to be floated, and the torrential rains and floods provided the lush green fodder which was the natural food for the elephants.

So, when May came and the rains had at last broken, I had to say goodbye to Jim; he went off by himself for a month's tour, his only companion Molly.

I was glad our house was away from the river. It was now fast becoming a tearing muddy swell; overflowing its banks and marooning the little thatched houses on stilts on a great lake of water. The native children were paddling happily about in boats between the houses, but for their parents, at this time, life must have been difficult in the extreme.

Mould began to grow on everything, and when I got my shoes out of the cupboard some of them looked as if they were made of fur. Everything one possessed and wore was sticky and damp.

The rain fell in heavy sheets for days on end. Then suddenly, like a tap turned off, it would cease and the sun would glare down again, drawing great clouds of steam out of the sodden earth. Only the insects revelled in these conditions, and in the first fortnight after the monsoon had broken, winged creatures seemed to come alive by the million.

One evening I looked across at the venetian blind which had been let down, and thought that a new one must have been fitted; instead of the usual dull-finished slats, the whole thing looked like glistening chain armour. When I got close to it, I saw that this was in reality a breathing seething mass of beetles and bugs.

Aung Net had gone off with Jim, so I called Po Lone, who had remained behind, to come and get rid of them somehow. He smiled superciliously at my discomfort and slowly lifted up the large oil lamp and carried it out into the garden, a swarm of insects following in his wake.

These long wet weeks when Jim was away could sometimes be depressing, and Po Lone certainly didn't help to cheer one up. He was extremely efficient and when we had returned from the jungle we found he had kept everything in wonderful order. But, as is so often the way with a bachelor's servant, he had taken none too well to having a woman running the house. Unlike Aung Net and Joseph, the cook, who shared with me all their allegiance to Jim, Po Lone was a townee, and perhaps this was the difference—none of his fellow servants seemed to have much use for him either.

He showed his disapproval in many pin-prick ways. Two small things especially stick in my memory. I had a lovely pair of fine grey silk stockings, which he took away and washed, and then brought back, looking like torn cobwebs. He came in, holding them up for me to see, with a silly smirk on his face. I was furious, but tried not to show it.

The second incident was connected with my jodhpurs. These were a very smart pair with doe-skin strappings, made in England by Chesters of Newmarket. I was very proud of these, and had often told him that they were never to be washed. Imagine my annoyance when sorting the laundry one day I found my lovely jodhpurs ruined.

Considering our washing was all done by beating the clothes on rocks in the local streams, it was no wonder they looked as they did. I was really irritated, and told Jim about it; after that, Po Lone seemed to bear me more of a grudge than ever. Jim had never really cared for him much himself, and told him if there was any more trouble he would have to go.

Jim had been gone about three weeks when one morning at about four o'clock I was startled out of my wits by hearing a gruff voice speaking from the bottom of my bed. I sat up, wondering who on earth it could be. Moonlight was streaming into the room through the verandah doors which were wide open, and after a moment or two I was able to distinguish our nightwatchman, Saw Noo. He was squatting at the end of my bed, his face peering through the white mosquito net, talking very gently so as not to frighten me.

"Thakinma, Thakinma. Come quickly," he said. "You must come. A messenger has arrived with a note from master."

"Well, bring it to me here, Saw Noo," I said.

"No, Thakinma, I cannot do that—the messenger insists he hands it to you himself."

My immediate reaction was fear, and I wondered if this could be a put-up job of some sort. But Saw Noo was so calm that I was persuaded it was no hoax, and got out of bed.

Downstairs, squatting on his haunches just inside the verandah door, was the messenger. His long hair was soaking wet and dripping onto his bare shoulders and he looked very weary. He handed me an envelope; the word *Urgent* was scrawled all over it in large red letters in Jim's writing.

I walked over and read the note inside by the light of the watchman's lamp, and was puzzled beyond words to read: "Do not eat or drink anything served by Po Lone, but prepare everything yourself. Am told he is putting poison pills in your food and drink. Shall start home right away."

I picked up a pencil, and in order to allay Jim's anxiety scribbled on the envelope: "Don't worry, am as fit as can be." I told the messenger to get this back to Jim as quickly as he could, and went back to bed, completely mystified.

Next morning I went over to the policeman's bungalow and told him the whole story. He said Po Lone must be got out of the servants' quarters at once, and that he would arrange to hold him on some pretext or other till Jim arrived.

I was certain Jim could not get back for at least three days, as I knew the country through which he would have to travel was practically impassable at this time of year. The journey could only be done in slow stages as the streams were now in full spate and at times it was impossible to cross them without being swept away. I could not help feeling anxious for him, and afraid that in his hurry he might take unnecessary risks.

His journey back was a story in itself—in fact, he has told it most graphically in one of his books. By some miracle, he managed to do this trek—which had taken him five days going out—in only forty-eight hours.

No one knew the ways of the jungle better than Jim, but he was always insistent that foolish risks should not be taken, and we never travelled at night. The country was infested with big game, and this was their hunting time. But Jim was so anxious to get on that he forgot all dangers and kept going night and day, struggling on without rest or sleep.

I was more than glad to see him when he got back, but horrified at what this journey had done to him. He looked quite unlike himself—utterly weary, and all he wanted to do was to sleep.

Next day Jim told Joseph to hand him the pills he had seen Po Lone dropping into my food. Joseph was in a great state, and quite certain, from conversations he had overheard, that Po Lone was trying to get rid of me.

Having calmed him down, Jim sent for Po Lone and taxed him with the story. I could see him from the verandah standing there with his head bent before Jim. As a rule the Burman never raises his voice, but now Po Lone was almost shouting in his hot denial.

The pills were shown to him. He looked Jim straight in the eye and said, "Very well, Thakin, if you do not believe me, I will eat one in front of you every day for a week."

Knowing the Burmese mentality, Jim was not convinced. He turned to the policeman, handed him the pills, and said, "Take Po Lone to the jetty and see that he leaves down-river on tomorrow's boat, for the first stage of his journey to Pyin-mana, his home town."

Po Lone raised his head and glared across at me. I felt that at that moment he would gladly have murdered me, even if he had not tried to do so before. We never saw him again, neither did we ever really get to the bottom of what had happened, as there was no one in Mawlaik who could analyse the pills.

The police thought that Po Lone, knowing that he was possibly going to be dismissed, may have thought up a plan to try to prevent this. They suggested that he might have been to the village sayah, or wise man, and asked him for some sort of charm to win us over. Having got the magic pills, he may have put them in my food for this purpose.

Everyone tried to persuade me that this was so, and it was certainly a more comforting theory than the slightly more dramatic one which I myself was inclined to believe.

Chapter XVII

THE DANCING THAKIN

CURIOUSLY enough, in spite of the excessively humid heat, rains and pests, we always looked back on our two years in Mawlaik as extremely happy ones. We were young and newly married, and difficulties slid away and were forgotten almost as soon as they arose. The variety of the life, too, suited both our temperaments.

Our long jungle tours were packed with interest and excitement, and Jim's love of elephants was infectious. I was beginning to be almost as intrigued by their intelligence and entertaining ways as he was, although I could not yet claim, as he did, to know each animal individually by personality and name. This was quite a feat anyway, as spread over his forest area there must have been well over a hundred animals working for the logging camps.

Returning to Mawlaik again from the jungle was a pleasant contrast—to sleep once more in our own bungalow, after months on end touring in dusty tents, seemed a luxury in itself.

As a reaction to getting back to comparative civilization again and meeting up with one's friends, life was apt to turn into a series of gay parties, often inspired by Jim. He was never happier than when he was ordering prairie oysters all round, or dancing into the small hours—any excuse for a party was seized upon.

Sometimes when we were miles away touring, we would come upon the Burmese villagers celebrating with a *pwé*. This they dearly loved to do, and whenever someone died, was married, divorced, or went into a monastery, one of these stage performances was always put on to mark the occasion. Even if a bullock was sold for an extra good price, this was reason enough. Whenever he saw festivities Jim always itched to take part himself.

Once, when we arrived at a jungle village, a *pwé* was put on to celebrate our coming. Jim and I were given places of honour—the only two chairs, set in front of all the squatting villagers and close to the stage.

I was a bit worried when I had settled in my seat as Jim seemed to have disappeared completely, and the show was about to begin. Eventually, they had to start without him.

Even in this remote village, the costumes were fabulously beautiful. The central characters, the prince and princess, were in court dress. They wore tight-fitting lace jackets, the stiff brocaded wings embroidered with gold and pearls, and high pagoda-like crowns. Brilliantly hued skirts were wound so tightly round their bottoms that one wondered how they could move at all. The whole stage was crowded with performers—a riot of silks and embroideries.

The play was under way, and still no Jim beside me—I began to feel embarrassed. Then I heard a soft murmuring and tittering amongst the crowd on the ground behind me. It grew louder as they rose to their feet, clapping, and shouting "Thakin gyi, thakin gyi!"—There he is, there he is!

Coming forward from the back of the stage, where he had been squatting unnoticed, was a figure dressed gorgeously like the others but with a big nose and quite a different shaped face—Jim's in fact.

The play was always spontaneous, and he came to the front of the platform, bowing to the princess, who was smiling shyly and turning her head slightly away. But with his wonderful understanding of the Burmese mind and his natural charm and humour, he soon won her over. She came forward gracefully, and they did a stately dance opposite each other, Jim quite unselfconscious and very serious all the while.

The crowd roared their approval.

After it was all over, the headman came up to me and said, "I used to know Thakin when he was here before—and how he would love to join in our celebrations—in fact we called him 'The Dancing Thakin'. I couldn't imagine him just sitting watching and not taking part, so I asked him to join in. He wouldn't let me tell you, as he wanted to give you a surprise."

Life could not have been happier, and it came as quite a jolt when the mail boat brought a letter one day to say that Mawlaik was no longer to be our headquarters. I had grown attached to our home, and we had redesigned the garden which, except in the hot weather, was ablaze with alamander, bougainvillaea and cannas. It was sad to think of leaving it for good.

We were to move from the wet zone to Shwebo, which is one of the driest places in Burma. Once there had been an Army station there, but owing to shortage of water they had had to move away. Our only consolation was that we knew a baby was on the way, and at least Shwebo was slightly more accessible and the climate a little more healthy.

"I am afraid it will be far too dry to be able to make a garden there," said Jim. "But what worries me most about this new posting is that the Company want me to go there all the way on foot, inspecting various forests en route. It will mean a five months' trek through the jungle, and I can't take you with me now." But we could neither of us bear the thought of being parted, and in the end I managed to persuade Jim that exercise would be the very best thing for me.

We set off together as soon as the rains had ceased, and everything was still lush and green as we walked up river. We were looking for a place where the Chindwin was narrow enough to cross, not so much for our sakes, for we would get the locals to ferry us over in their boats, but for our elephants who had to swim.

This was no hardship to them, for they were strong swimmers and one could almost feel their exhilaration when the baggage was unloaded from their backs and they were able to wade in. I loved watching them as, when they first entered rivers of any depth, they would always feel their way very carefully by plunging their trunks into the deep mud, and reconnoitring the ground beneath. When they were satisfied there was a firm foothold, they slowly moved forward, looking rather unwieldy, usually led by a young one. Once in the water and able to swim, they were perfectly at home.

Jim was often asked how far exactly an elephant could swim. When he had been in the Andamans he had been able to prove that it is at least two miles—an elephant had swum that distance between two islands—and this was in the open sea.

They were able to take such rivers as the Chindwin at this time of year easily in their stride; and now, as they plunged in, they looked as though they meant to enjoy it. Being large and buoyant, an elephant if he wants can emerge high out of the water as he swims, but what he really likes is to sink himself right underneath, leaving only the tip of his trunk sticking up, like a periscope, to breathe through.

The oozies on the elephants' backs were having a tricky time trying to stay put. It was quite an exciting performance for them, and they had even taken bets among themselves as to who would sit it out the longest.

The usual intuitive relationship with their elephants seemed more acute than ever now. Somehow they were able to feel by the animal's breathing when it was about to submerge, and would take as deep a breath as possible themselves and go under the water with their mounts. Sometimes both oozie and elephant would completely disappear underneath the water for a few seconds, the oozie eventually bobbing up like a champagne cork, unable to hang on any longer.

We always thought that the elephant knew that he had the power to stay submerged just that much longer than a man, and enjoyed the joke of being, for once, one up on his rider—or rather, one down.

The river, though, was stronger even than the elephants, and the currents carried some of them off course down stream and they landed in twos and threes on the opposite bank, coming out of the water like sedate old gentlemen, standing there patiently till their oozies caught up with them again.

*   *   *

We were to have a real worry during the week that followed.

Molly, who as a rule was so alert and game for anything, had not been herself for several days. Instead of keeping a watchful eye on every movement that Jim made, she seemed uninterested and dreamy, and did not even care for her food much. We neither of us dared mention the dreaded word 'rabies', although it began to be uppermost in both our minds.

Jim made an early start one morning to do a day's prospecting in the jungle, taking Molly with him. I stayed behind and tortured myself all day, wondering how I could broach the subject of her illness when he got back. Of one thing I was sure—if she were no better, the moment had now come when we must discuss it. I loved Molly, but to Jim she meant something so deep that I could hardly imagine him without her.

The day seemed long, and towards evening I started out through the trees to meet him. As he walked up to camp, I noticed at once that Molly wasn't with him. There was no need for words—I knew what had happened.

He told me afterwards that it had been one of the most awful decisions of his life. Alone that day, he had been trying to make up his mind what to do when he had noticed Molly looking towards him with glazed eyes, as though she did not know him.

He tied her up for a while, but when he set her free again, a wild look came into her face and she went padding round and round in circles. He felt terribly distressed, but for the first time in his life he also felt afraid of her. The decision had been made for him—with aching heart, he loaded his gun and shot her.

I never saw Jim morose at any time, and even now, as

we moved on and our thoughts were with this much-loved dog, whom we had to leave behind us in the jungle, we talked of other things.

Molly had brought us together, and now her death was a sorrow silently shared.

CHAPTER XVIII

THROUGH THE TEAK FORESTS

OUR five months' trek between Mawlaik and Shwebo was for Jim part of his job. His work all centred on the extraction of teak from these forests, and as we went along he was able to explain to me a little of what this entailed.

Long ago it had been realised that if timber firms like the Bombay Burmah Teak Corporation were allowed into the jungle to extract the valuable trees just when and how they liked, the accessible parts of the country would naturally be worked first. Serious harm would be done, as these parts of the jungle would soon become denuded of trees.

In order to avoid this, the whole country had been divided into areas, each area being again subdivided into compartments, and these were leased to the various timber companies.

The teak tree often grew in the most inaccessible places where no machines could possibly reach it; it would hardly have been economic to use machines in such conditions in any case. This is why elephants were used—they were capable of pushing their way through almost impenetrable terrain, which sometimes hung thick with every kind of ropey tangled creeper. They could also climb up the precipitous ravine to reach the odd tree growing perilously at the top.

It was calculated that a teak tree increased in girth approximately half an inch a year, and it was only mature enough for felling when its girth measured over seven feet six inches— a foot less in the dry zone. The Forest Department ruled that only dead teak should be extracted, and they did the killing themselves by girdling the bark of all trees of these measurements.

This in itself might sound a fairly simple job, but teak grows very sparsely; often only one or two trees to the acre. The exploration of each compartment, then girdling trees of suitable size, numbering them, and plotting their whereabouts on a map, was a considerable operation.

The golden rule when carrying out this work, so that all the ground was covered, was that neither a stream nor a ridge must be crossed. The Forest Officer and his team of Burmans would start from the mouth of a stream and work upwards, spreading themselves out fanwise between the stream and the nearest ridge. Each man carried a strip of pliable bamboo, cut to either 7 ft. 6 in. or 6 ft. 6 in. lengths, depending on the type of forest they were exploring, and whenever one of them came to a teak tree, he wrapped his bamboo strip round it at chest height. If the ends did not meet, he knew the tree was the correct size, and he would call the Forest Officer to mark it for girdling. After this, it was numbered serially and carefully plotted on a map.

All this sounds easy, but in the hilly jungle country of Burma, and working in the steamy sweating heat, it was extremely arduous. One moment a tree might have to be examined low down at stream level, and the next another one growing at the top of a high and difficult ridge would have to be inspected. The job involved ranging for miles, climbing up and down precipitous country, often having to hack through thick jungle as well. The Forest Officers certainly earned their pay.

When exploration and girdling were completed, the compartment was shut for three years, and the timber firms were not allowed to do any felling before this time was up. This ensured that the trees were properly killed and had had time to dry out enough to allow them to float downstream to the mills.

The teak firms then came in. They placed all the responsibility on the shoulders of an Assistant working a particular area. His job was to make estimates of how many men were required for the felling, how much food, in the form of rice, sugar, dried fish, etc., each camp would require, and how much money was needed to pay for all this.

Jim said that when he was an Assistant he took a supply of opium as well, as many of the jungle Burmans who undertook the felling and logging work were opium eaters. They had become so used to it that it was a necessity to them, and if a supply was not available, they would just leave work and go in search of it.

Then there was the task of estimating how many elephants would be needed for the dragging work. Each elephant of course had his oozie to help him, and many of these would bring their wives along with them. These all had to be fed and looked after, and medical supplies had to be arranged for them, as well as for the elephants.

The fellers required saws, axes, felling wedges, saw sets and sharpening tools. The elephants required harness, dragging chains, earth oil, tamarind, and a host of other supplies; and the staff would require pay. So that on opening up a compartment, the Forest Assistant had a large job of estimating and accounting on his hands.

Apart from all this, he would have to explore the whole area to decide the best and easiest drag routes for his elephants, where to site camps and timber depots, and many other details, including finding a suitable place for his own jungle hut. Soon the work would get started, and out of apparent chaos order would emerge, and the work of extraction would be carried out.

The Forest Assistant was responsible for all the logging, and once again every tree in the compartment had to be marked to show, this time, how the logs were to be cut. Great care had to be taken, as a log cut wrongly could lose more than half its value.

After extraction, the Assistant had to visit every stump, to ensure that no timber was left behind. When it was finally cleared, the area was closed and not touched again for thirty years. During this time the remaining young teak trees were able to grow up, while the more mature ones carried out their normal process of seeding, and continuity was ensured.

On the way to Shwebo we many times came across the narrow paths that wild elephants had made as they wandered through the jungle; and sometimes Jim would point out a tiny teak sapling sprouting in one of their footprints. The pocket of soil in the indentation was a perfect place for a seed to rest in and grow—a little protected from the wind and with the earth already loosened to receive the roots. Most of the trees had started their life nursed in the footprint of some wild animal.

We came upon giant trees, too; some girdled and dead, their bare branches looking like the blanched upstretched bones of a huge skeleton against the green of the surrounding forest. They were numbered and ready for felling.

Jim put his hand on the smooth bole of one of these. "This tree, at least a hundred and fifty years old and looking so desolate and forgotten," he said, "will soon take up life again— perhaps as the deck of a luxury yacht, or a large ship, or maybe just a garden seat standing waiting to be sold in some country shop in England. Its wood is unique, and has incomparable qualities—it is durable, will not warp, and no nail will rust in it."

* * *

Burma carries a vast fortune which nature has provided— acres and acres of forest scattered with valuable teak, but in years gone by, the Burman has never been able to fully exploit this natural wealth.

He is by nature unambitious, and his religion teaches him that to have sufficient to meet everyday needs is the ideal state of affairs. This is all he strives for, and he never had the inclination or ability to bring into practice the complexities of conserving and extracting the trees.

Some day perhaps he may wake out of his lethargy and

rise to the occasion, but I think with his temperament it is unlikely. Since the Second World War the foreign timber companies have all gone, and he does own and run his forests, but as far as I know there is no methodical plan for working the timber, and at the present time the export of teak is down to a minimum.

Jim loved the story of the development of the teak forests and the lives of the men who worked in them, but his elephants interested him even more. It was their achievements in wrestling the timber from almost inaccessible places, and their never failing hard-working patience, that inspired him most of all.

It was they who made the whole enterprise possible. From the men it required stamina and discipline and calculating brains; but the elephants gave their unswerving obedience to man's commands, and their huge strength to hauling the logs which man alone could not move.

Above all, it was their judgment when manœuvring these unwieldy objects that counted—that sixth sense of knowing exactly whether a delicate touch here, or a mighty push there, would secure the desired result.

"We owe it to each one of them," Jim would say, "to see that he enjoys life and is never overburdened. It may sometimes mean a little sacrifice on our part, but all the teak in Burma would be of no avail if he were not there to extract it for us."

CHAPTER XIX

THE PYTHON IN THE POOL

WE had been travelling for several weeks and were now in deep evergreen jungle passing through wild unexplored country. At times our progress was very slow as we had to cut our way through a maze of trailing lengths of cane.

Nature seems to have designed the evils as well as the good. This cane, for instance, with ground-growing tendrils over a hundred feet in length had, every three or four feet, a barb like a trout hook. It was worse than barbed wire to walk through, as it tore at one's legs and clothes. If one of the dogs got caught in it, he had the sense not to struggle, seeming by some instinct to know that he would only get more tied up.

There was a particular kind of bamboo, too, which caused us lots of discomfort. When touched it would shower off a fine powdery dust which, if it got into the opening of a shirt, was worse than the schoolboy's itch powder; in fact, we often used to say that this must have been its origin. The Burman had a good cure for it. He would let down his long oily hair and use it as a sort of brush.

As a child in England soon learns to avoid a stinging nettle, so a jungle man would avoid the petya in Burma. But this was no ordinary stinging-nettle—it grew to six feet and was often used by game or a wounded animal who knew it as a protection from a following hunter. Ten minutes amongst a growth of it caused a few days of unbearable irritation and fever. I once walked into a bush of petya and it was not until I got back into camp that I felt as though a thousand hairy caterpillars were crawling all over me. I was covered from head to foot in white weals and had a hellish night—nothing I did seemed to help the irritation.

There was a creeper in the jungle which we had to be particularly careful to avoid. It was called the suyit and was often to be found growing right across our path. In order to pass, it had to be slashed with a knife, and as soon as it was cut, a white milky sap oozed out. If this should get splashed into an eye, it could cause a form of ophthalmia which would develop into an opalescence similar to a cataract. As we cut our way through, the elephants' heads were very close to the torn undergrowth and great care had to be taken.

Jim had had one female elephant completely blinded in both eyes through the juice of this creeper. She had a young calf about five years old, and he noticed one day, to his astonishment, that the calf was leading its mother by carrying her trunk on its back. Jim gave strict instructions that that calf was never to be trained for work, but to be left with its mother. It continued to lead her until it unfortunately died in a tragic way when a river bank subsided and buried it under the water. Not long afterwards the mother, pining inconsolably for her little guide elephant, died too.

It was a law of the jungle man that the surface of the blade of the knife was turned over to tap the sharp edge of creepers to blunt them. The pointed edge of certain bamboos could penetrate like a shot arrow if merely walked against. In spite of all precautions there were many painful wounds on this account. A man we had known was so damaged in the groin by such a bamboo that he had to be invalided out of the forest service.

It was a relief to drop down into the creeks where the going was easier. These were dank and dark, with sheer sides of smooth black rock thirty or forty feet high. Water constantly dripped and trickled down the shiny surface, making mysterious deep pools in the gorge below.

I took a stick and was idly stirring the water in one of these pools when some large prawns emerged from under the weeds. Both our thoughts immediately turned to seaside teas in England, and I was delighted when Jim said they were quite edible. I settled down to catch as many as I could with my hands, and we ate them for supper that evening, delectably cooked by Joseph.

We both delighted, like children, in dabbling about in these miniature lagoons—they were deliciously cool after the heat of the jungle. Jim was fishing about in one of them when he called over to me to look at something he had caught.

He was holding up in his fingers what appeared to be a piece of yellowy-green string, and I imagined it was a bit of weed of some sort. He tied it into loose knots and then replaced it in the shallow water. Without any struggle, it slowly untied itself—I was fascinated.

"It's called a *yay shin*," he said, "and the Burmans always say that one must not drink water in which it is found—which is probably good sense."

I had often heard the Burmese referring to a *nat shin*, one of their spirits which was supposed to be like a huge serpent, and I imagine this was where the idea originated.

These ravines were a botanist's paradise. The maidenhair fern adorning the rocks hung like delicate green lace from top to bottom of the cliff, and trailing festoons of brilliant carmine small-flowered begonias shed their blossoms amongst it. In the stream bed itself I found a plant with a flower of the purest blue shaped like a star; I collected roots of this and many others, which I hoped I might get to grow in our garden in Shwebo—although this would be a pretty hopeless task, by all accounts.

It was in one of these streams that I saw my first snake of any size. We were walking up the gorge to where it was opening out a little, and the sun was able to filter through, when we heard a shout of alarm from one of the Burmese jungle followers coming up behind us; so we turned and went back to see what was the matter.

There, resting on a gnarled tree root at the edge of a pool, was the head of a snake. The Burman had mistaken it for a water tortoise and had just bent down to pick it up, thinking it would be a choice morsel for his evening curry. As he stretched his hand towards it, he had seen the flickering tongue and knew it was a snake.

Jim stopped the elephants to acquire his rifle, and standing on the shingle beside the stream he fired at close range and blew the creature's head to pieces.

Then, to my horror, its writhing body rose like a whip-lash, coil after coil out of the pool—seventeen feet of it as we afterwards found out, and as thick as a man's thigh. The python, for that is what it was, had been lying there, probably asleep, hidden beneath the water through which Jim and I had walked only a moment or two before.

As we watched, the headless monster then wriggled back again into the pool—it was uncanny. The Burmans pulled it out onto the sand again, but once more it slithered back.

Not until sundown did the nerves of its great body finally die, and as we all stood round and looked at it we noticed that halfway down its length was a big bulge. "It's obviously swallowed an animal of some sort," said Jim. "I hope to goodness it isn't a dog—it's just about that size."

But the bulge was no dog—as the Burmans cut it open, they uncovered a barking deer, complete with horns, skin—everything. Having seen the python's small, pear-shaped head, I was astonished that, even though it seemed to have no hinge in its lower jaw, it could swallow anything as large as this.

When attacking a largish animal—and even a calf will not daunt it—the python first makes for the head. Then in a flash it coils itself tightly round the body, releasing its grip only when the animal has stopped struggling and it knows that life has been crushed out of it. The snake then holds its victim firmly by coiling its tail round the body, and proceeds to cover the head with thick saliva to make it slippery.

The animal is then forced slowly down its throat and into its stomach—the tiny jaws having been able to expand wide enough to swallow something of this size, unbelievable though it may seem.

When the Burman first saw this python I think he may have shouted more from surprise than fear, as their bite is not poisonous and they do not generally attack man, unlike the hamadryad or king cobra. Nevertheless, any snake at first sight is always treated with caution, and these gigantic pythons, with their enormous strength, have many legendary tales woven round them.

Its skin was scraped and then laced onto a bamboo frame to dry. Later, Jim sent it to India to be cured, and although many people tried to persuade me to have belts or shoes made out of the lovely grey and white skin, I somehow did not want to. I kept it as it was, and still have it to this day, rolled up in a cupboard in my house in Cornwall.

* * *

Lovely as the gorges in the jungle creeks were at this time of year, they caused many a problem where the working of the timber was concerned. In the narrowest places, hundreds of logs and debris were likely to get stuck, having been brought down earlier in the year when the water was in full spate. Now they were left lying marooned in a tangled mass, waiting for the elephants to come and sort them out.

Jim had planned to inspect one of these gorges en route, and when we arrived the elephants were hard at work trying to get the logs straightened out. Some of the timber was so tightly jammed that even they could not manage to move it without the help of a block and pulley wheel.

A wire hawser was stretched right across the gorge with a pulley wheel in the centre, a rope passing over this, attached at one end to the jammed log and at the other to the elephant.

"Pull, pull!" the oozie cried. The elephant lunged forward, straining with all his power against his breast strap. There was a sound of creaking and splintering wood—the log had shifted an inch or two—then it jammed again.

It was a slow, laborious job, but eventually it was worked free, the oozie congratulating his animal as it finally came away. There were about five elephants working in this ravine, and I noticed the incessant monologue each oozie poured out on his animal—it seemed to be an essential part of the proceedings.

The work was very arduous, and must have been disheartening. It would sometimes take months to straighten out the chaos, and then, when another river rise came, the same thing happened all over again—the logs building up in the very same place.

We moved on, making little headway, and at times seemed to be hemmed in on every side. This was the only time I had ever been with Jim when he completely lost his bearings.

It was the elephants that worried him most. We could have camped anywhere, but they had to be near water. Our only form of guidance was the compartment numbers blazed on trees, and in some cases these had grown into the trunks and were indecipherable.

The oozies began to get silent, a sure sign they were apprehensive. Then, after several hours' very slow going, we were climbing towards the top of a high ridge when there came a shout of joy from one of the men who was just ahead. He had suddenly spotted the Mu river in the distance, and knew this would give Jim his bearings.

All the elephant men broke into song, so overwhelmed with relief did they feel. We knew at last where we were, and could now drop down into the valley below us and camp for the night.

The site had to be prepared on arrival, and was very rough and ready compared with what we had had earlier on. No clean bamboo floors—just a tarpaulin laid over the roughly cleared ground, and the tent pitched on this. As we were in wild elephant country, we had the fire made near the entrance to our tent instead of, as was usual, in the middle of the clearing.

It was difficult to get off to sleep because as soon as dark fell there were constant explosions, like rockets going off, coming from where the Burmans were camped nearby.

"Drat those oozies," said Jim. "They are burning green bamboos. We shall have to listen to this until their fires burn down."

The Burmans love to shove these green bamboos into their fire at night, and get as much joy out of the resulting bangs as a schoolboy letting off jumping crackers. They did it ostensibly to frighten away wild animals and give themselves courage—but it was more than that, and became an entertainment in itself.

When the thick green bamboo stalk entered the hot embers of the fire, the cool air in the hollow segments expanded and they burst with a sound like rifle fire. At each explosion there would be a whoop of joy from the oozies, as they sat round exchanging gossip and gambling together late into the night.

In these out-of-the-way places, not only did one lose one's whereabouts, but also all sense of time. Jim had set off one morning early to arrange for the removing of some timber which had got stuck in deep sand owing to a river changing its course and leaving it stranded. I had decided to have a day in camp, and rest.

After he had gone I thought I would write some letters, but could not remember the date so I got out my diary to work it out. It was only then that I realised it was Christmas Day—both of us had completely forgotten.

When Jim came back, I rushed up and gave him a whacking kiss and said, "Happy Christmas, darling!"

He looked at me in blank amazement and said, "Can't be true!"

"It is," I said. "Shows how wrapped up in those old elephants of yours you are!"

We both roared with laughter, and had an extra gin that night to make up for the oversight.

CHAPTER XX

WHEN SORROWS COME

We had left Mawlaik early in November and arrived in Shwebo in March. The countryside was like a desert; what once had been grass crinkled like cinders beneath our feet. Dust was everywhere.

I asked to see the garden—there was no garden. A desolate compound, the only growing things about half a dozen frangipani trees, which were leafless and grotesque in shape, with leper-like stunted branches.

Once, early on, I had been through this place in the train with Uncle Pop. We had had to halt here for about ten minutes, and I remember saying to him, "Surely no Europeans live in this dreadful spot?"

It had struck me then as hot, dirty, dry and derelict, and I should not have liked to think that later on it was to be my home for seven years.

But, since I had been married to Jim, I really didn't care where his work sent us. As long as we were sharing life together, it seemed good wherever it was. For me he was the perfect companion. Most people, however close to them one becomes, have a barrier somewhere beyond which it is impossible to cross. There was nothing like this with Jim. I could talk to him as if I were talking to myself. Sometimes, indeed, he would know what I was thinking before I spoke, and I suspect it was this sensitive perception which made him so at one with animals.

We were glad that almost as soon as we arrived at Shwebo we were due for leave in England. We were much looking forward to the break, and were pleased that our baby was to be born at home. But as it turned out, the year that followed was, I think, the unluckiest in all our life together—nothing seemed to go right.

Six weeks after we got back our son Jeremy was born in Penzance—he was a lovely, robust baby. In the meanwhile, Jim had been none too well; his long years in the jungle, with constant bouts of malaria and other diseases, had caught up with him. The company advised him to go into the Hospital for Tropical Diseases for treatment while he was in England.

He had been there only a week when Jeremy picked up a virulent flu germ, and died quite suddenly. It was a terrible shock to us. We both loved, and wanted, children.

The leave was a sad one, softened only by the fact that we saw our families again; but even this was marred for Jim, as his father had died about six months before our homecoming.

* * *

We returned to Shwebo feeling very lost. It was by no means a welcoming place; we lived in what had been the officers' quarters of the old military establishment—five miles out of the ugly town—but even here the surroundings looked bare and thirsty for water.

What had been the mess was now Jim's office and also housed the unmarried assistants when they came in for leave from the jungle. Our house had been the major's bungalow, and our servants were now expected to live in what had been his servants' quarters. These were in poor repair and very cramped, and Jim was not at all happy about them. Later he saw to it that they were pulled down and rebuilt.

The old barracks stood empty and forlorn, and the little military cemetery nearby was a sad memorial to many young soldiers who, unable to stand the climate, had died in Shwebo in the past. I noticed that the average age carved on their

tombstones was about twenty-one—fevers and dysentery had
taken their toll.

But all this had happened many years ago, at the end of
the last century. Things were better now, and the treatment
for these diseases had advanced considerably; also, there were
fewer of us, so the shortage of water was not felt so acutely.
Even so, every drop had to be brought to us each day in great
barrels drawn by a bullock cart from a well two and a half
miles away.

For our first year, I was to be the only Englishwoman in
the place—it was an entirely bachelor station. This did not
worry me much, although it could be quite lonely on occasions when Jim was away on tour.

Shwebo—the name means golden chief—was the birthplace
and burial site of Alaung Paya, the founder of the last dynasty
of Burmese kings. These kings had imported convict labour
to build the famous Shwebo canal system, and as a result it
was always said that the scum of Burma was still to be found
living in this district. It was true that there were a number of
dacoits and outlaws about, and one of the first things Jim did
was to have a trap-door made and fitted over the open stairway, so that we could have the security of locking up at night.

When we returned from leave, the place looked perhaps
slightly less parched than when we had first arrived and, in
order to take my mind off my troubles, I decided to get down
to trying to grow something. An Indian who had worked in
the garden at Mawlaik had come here with us, and he encouraged me to get going.

His mentality was extremely simple and he had been rather
rudely nicknamed 'Pugli'—meaning idiot—by his friends.
But as far as his gardening went, he was far from being an idiot.
He made things grow under almost impossible conditions, and
cared for his flowers as if they were his children. I would
see him, on the rare occasions when we did have rain, paddling
round under his old umbrella, shaking water off the heads

of the sunflowers and other heavy blooms so that they would not snap off.

Pugli taught me much, and it was a delight to watch the care he took over planting the seeds, and the way he nurtured the seedlings, too. Everything matured here so much more quickly than in England—it was like raising plants in an incubation frame. I can remember scarlet geraniums, planted from seed, growing into quite large plants and flowering in less than three months.

Jim, too, although he hardly knew one plant from another, became very keen and had lots of ideas. He arranged for an extra water supply to fill large earthenware jars which were sunk in the ground near the flower beds, and even designed a sunken garden to make the place look less flat.

Gradually, the barren waste round our house grew into an almost show-garden, full of orange and red cassia bushes, pink and white hibiscus and magenta bougainvillaea. Pugli even managed to get a morning glory creeper to run riot over our porch, and its fresh brilliant blue flowers delighted us every day.

After a while, rich Burmans used to bring their families out in cars for a joy-ride in the evenings in order to peer through the gate and look at it. Pugli was immensely proud, and so were we.

But it was poor Pugli's love of flowers that led to his undoing. A Burmese neighbour nearby was also endeavouring to make a garden, and had found a native worker called Mahmoud to help her with it. Pugli kept a close eye on all that was going on, and took a great delight in telling me how much better our garden was than theirs.

However, one day he came to me looking rather depressed and said, "Mahmoud is getting his garden to look almost as good as mine, Memsahib, and what is more I am certain he is stealing my seedlings."

Nothing I could do would cheer him up or make him think otherwise, and as time went on he became more and more

In the cool of the evening — the day's work done

Unloading stores beside the Chindwin

They push

And they pull

obsessed about the other garden, and even began to lose enthusiasm for his own. To add to his troubles, some stray bullocks one day broke through the fence and trampled all over the flower beds before they were finally chased out. This put Pugli in a towering rage, and he went out and got blind drunk.

That evening Jim found him wandering round the garden trying to put it to rights. He was muttering to himself, "Mahmoud did this to spite me—he did it on purpose," and as he stumbled about, very much the worse for drink, he was doing even more damage than had already been done. Jim was very angry, and sent him back to his quarters.

Next morning Pugli was abject. He came to the verandah, where we were sitting, his long hair, which was usually in a tight knot on top of his head, hanging raggedly over his face. He knelt at my feet, and then kissed them; it was his way of saying how sorry he was.

I was terribly embarrassed, and begged Jim to tell him he was forgiven and to go back to his garden. "Never let me see you in that state again," said Jim, "or you will have to go."

One morning our neighbour arrived and asked to speak to me. "Has Pugli any news of Mahmoud?" she said. "He hasn't been to work in the garden for two days. I have been over to his quarters to look for him, and asked everybody, but no one seems to have seen him. He can't have gone far because his things are exactly as he left them—even his money is there."

Pugli, however, was unable to throw any light on the matter, but in the days that followed he became more and more morose and we would catch him sitting staring into space, absolutely uninterested in everything.

The body of poor Mahmoud was found a week later—he had drowned in the well. When this was discovered, everyone was most concerned and upset, as he was a nice character and everybody liked him. Jim sent out to the garden to tell Pugli the sad news; but he was quite unconcerned, and continued watering without even turning round.

From that day onwards his brain seemed to get much worse. Jim and I looked out one night just after we had gone upstairs to bed, and saw him sitting in the moonlight under his open umbrella, as still as a statue. "He's quite cuckoo, poor chap," said Jim.

And that is what the police thought when they came to question him later—he was hardly able to talk sense to them. The death was a puzzle to everybody. It was only Jim and I who knew of the deep professional jealousy that had warped poor Pugli's mind.

"If we can get him home to India and his own family, that will be the best thing for him now," said Jim.

I was sad to see him go. As he drove off in the native pony cart he looked a forlorn figure, sitting bolt upright, clutching his rusty black umbrella, and with a tin box containing all he possessed on the seat beside him.

He hardly said goodbye to Jim or myself, but as they trotted away we both saw him turn his head and give one last look at the garden which had been his life for so long, and in the end his downfall.

CHAPTER XXI

THE LITTLE JUNGLE WALLAH

JIM's love of children, which was always returned in full
measure, was a profound thing. He had that rare quality
of being able to see things from a child's point of view. I
have seen children, known for their awkwardness and shyness
with adults, completely at ease with him.

He saw things as they did, and they would become voluble
and expressive in his company. Part of the reason for this
stemmed from a belief which he often expressed—that he
learned more from the young than he ever taught them.

To older children he gave confidence because he could
truthfully tell them he had been in more scrapes than they
could imagine. He was completely understanding of the
ambitions, temptations, pitfalls, and all the difficulties of youth.

I knew he had always looked forward to having children of
his own, and that the loss of our baby had been a terrible blow
to him. So that when, after two and a half years in Shwebo,
our second son was born he was welcomed with extra joy.

We both felt inordinately proud of him, and sometimes could
hardly believe it was true when we saw him sitting in his
pram amongst the flowers in our garden, and even in this un-
suitable climate looking as happy and healthy as though he
had been living in England.

I was determined, however, that his arrival was not going to
prevent Jim and me being together, and that as soon as the
time came we should all three go on tour in the jungle again.
I had loved those tours and could never understand how so
many of the wives in Burma, once they had families, were

content to stay in headquarters while their husbands went off. As a result, they were parted for more than half the year.

They probably thought that we were foolish and running unnecessary risks by taking our child with us, so far away from medical help. But, all in all, we felt the risk was worth it, especially as I had been lucky enough to find an exceptional little Karen girl to come and look after him.

Her name was Naw Lah and she was neat, petite and capable. Although she came from a jungle village, she was rather apprehensive, as most villagers were, of touring in the jungle itself. However, she adored Treve, our son, and would never have let him go without her.

When he was about fourteen months old, I started busily planning for him to accompany us. Jim got a local Chinese carpenter to make him a teak-framed cot which had latticed bamboo sides and was to serve as a bed, carry-cot, and playpen all in one—and was light enough to be slung on a centre bamboo pole and carried by two Burmans when we moved from camp to camp. Extra dried milk was added to our stores, and he even had a little topee like ours to wear on his head.

Jim and I were in the garden one day soon after the special carrier cot arrived, having fun on the lawn trying it out with Treve, when two Burmans came round the bungalow carrying something on their shoulders slung on a pole. As they came towards us, grinning from ear to ear, Jim recognised them as two forest men who had worked for him, and we saw that it was a leopard they were carrying, hung upside down by its feet.

"A present for 'The Baba'," they said—"to make a rug for him to crawl on." Treve took one look at the dead leopard, and started to bawl his head off; and my spaniel Rhoda, whom I had lately bought, shook all over, her hair standing on end—then bolted away and did not reappear until next day.

Meanwhile, Jim and I were thanking the Burmans as best we could for their present. They went away unperturbed, and still smiling. "I hope Treve's dislike of his new toy isn't a bad omen for his introduction to the jungle," said Jim, "but I don't suppose he is likely to see a leopard again, anyway."

It certainly did not prove a bad omen; Treve was a real 'jungle wallah' even at this age. He loved his mode of transport and more often than not had one of the cats or dogs as a fellow passenger. He was a most adaptable child and did not mind where he fed, and if the tents had not arrived, he would often have his bath out in the open under the trees. It was an exciting life for a child—there was always something new to interest him.

Naw Lah walked beside him or, if weary, had an occasional ride on Nicky, Jim's white pony. She was never at a loss for something to amuse him, and was most knowledgeable on all the things that grew in the jungle. She soon started to impress on him what he could or could not touch, and what he must not eat. Although I must say our faith in her knowledge did not extend to our sharing in the curries she made, to which she would add the queerest jungle fungi which she had gathered on the march.

When he grew to about three years old, Treve would ride instead of being carried. One of the Assistants had given him a pretty little skewbald pony which looked exactly like a circus horse.

Jim loved Treve dearly, and was always showing or teaching him something of jungle lore; in consequence, he became very advanced for his age. At three years old he could wield a Burmese dah, or jungle knife, with great ease although the blade was almost as big as he was. He was most determined and venturesome, but the jungle *nats* were on our side and he never came to any harm.

At home in Shwebo, too, as Treve grew older, he thoroughly enjoyed the life. In the East a child is loved by all, and everything is done for 'The Baba', as he or she is called, and one of our problems was to prevent Treve from getting spoilt. Quite a few married people had arrived in the station, bringing their families with them, which was company for him. None of the children seemed to mind the heat, provided they could get away to the hills once a year for a change.

From the very earliest days it was obvious he had inherited his father's great feeling for animals, and soon he was surrounded by pets. One was a peacock, taller than himself, and they became inseparable. The bird would even let Treve pick it up and carry it about under his arm. Another was Rikki, a little hog deer that Jim had rescued in the jungle from some Burmans who did not know what to do with her. She was the most beautiful little animal, a miniature deer so small that she was often completely hidden in the foot-high brown dry grass that grew in the compound where she was quite free to wander at will.

At first I fed her from a baby's bottle. She became quite accustomed to the dogs, and I was able to take her for short walks with them; during these she would keep close in against my legs—she almost adopted me as her mother. We let her run everywhere, and she and Treve were the greatest friends; she would come when we whistled, and take food from our hands when we were having tea on the verandah. She had a special protector too in Mirzah Khan, our night watchman, who would often come over even when off duty during the day, just to see how she was getting on. He really loved her.

But she had a sad end. An Assistant of Jim's came into our garden one morning, his brindle bull-terrier following him. Rikki, who had no fear of dogs, ran forward to greet them. It was all over in a snap—Mirzah Khan, who was standing near, ran forward to try to save her, but she had gone. He carried her to me in his arms, his eyes full of tears. "Poor, poor butcha (baby) . . ." he said.

Mirzah Khan was a Mahommedan—the only one amongst our staff—and he took his religion very seriously; it was nothing unusual to see him at sundown kneeling on his prayer mat in the garden, making obeisance to his God. He was high caste, and as we walked by in the evening if by chance our shadows should fall on his food, which did happen once or twice, it became unclean, and he was not allowed to eat it.

It was he who showed me the first Russel's viper I had ever seen. This is one of the most deadly of snakes—one bite from its poison fangs and a man is dead in less than twenty minutes.

He had been doing his nightly rounds when one of these ugly-looking creatures slid across his path—I heard him give a cry and saw him hit something with his stave. Luckily he managed to kill it; it was about two feet long, and a muddy dark brown, blunt at both ends and with no distinguishable head or tail.

Next day Mirzah Khan hunted everywhere in the garden for its mate which he knew would be around somewhere, and he eventually found it in a heap of brushwood that Pugli had piled in a corner. It shook us all, as this was the very spot where only the day before Treve had been happily playing, building himself a little house out of sticks.

We were delighted that Treve always seemed quite fearless and were determined not to fuss him into being afraid—nevertheless things like this made us a little anxious as we watched him running unconcernedly about the place.

Shwebo had many snakes; they would come out at dusk and after a shower of rain; and we never walked out at night without a light for fear of stepping on one. I have often heard frogs actually screaming with fright, too terrified to move as they were hypnotized by a snake that was just about to swallow them. Tree snakes, too, would climb up as far as the eaves of the bungalow—but they were quite harmless, except to the roosting sparrows who were a tasty meal.

Chapter XXII

THE TUSKERS SAVE THE BRIDGE

WHEN war broke out in September 1939 we were still in Shwebo. I find it hard now to believe what little impact the news made on us. Our lives were so remote from all that had been going on in Europe that it was extremely difficult to feel part of it. Nobody imagined in those early days how much it was soon to affect every one of us. For the first two years the East was strangely untroubled, though from the beginning Jim was deeply perturbed. I remember at a dinner party here in Shwebo how angry he got at the complacent conversation.

"You all sit here like ostriches," he said. "Your heads buried in the sands of wishful thinking. I tell you here and now that we shall all soon be deeply involved."

He was laughed to scorn and told not to be such a pessimist, but I have often wondered how many members of that party must have remembered his words when later they had to make their fearful, muddy exodus from Burma.

Jim would have liked to return to England, but he was told that for the moment he must carry on where he was, as his work was of national importance, that teak was as valuable towards the war effort as steel.

So a couple of months later we set off on tour in the jungle as originally arranged. We took Treve with us as usual and, as it happened, this time we narrowly escaped from quite a dangerous situation.

We were on the move from one camp to another. It was a

strangely grey day, and suddenly heavy drops started to fall. We were all very surprised as at this time of year, in January, rain was quite unheard of. It began to come down steadily and eventually became a downpour. We were totally unprepared, but the oozies did their best to protect our baggage on the elephants' backs by spreading tarpaulins right over it. Another small one was hung over the pole which carried Treve's cot, and he thought it was a huge joke, but the rest of us were beginning to get unpleasantly wet.

I remember poor old Joseph trudging along, the drips of rain falling from his little black fez down his face and dropping off the end of his nose. He managed a smile, but we wondered how he would get on when it came to lighting a fire and cooking in the rain.

It continued to pour, and Jim was getting worried. "We have got quite a wide river ahead of us to cross," he said, "and if it goes on like this there will be a rise and it will be impossible to get through. We must try and get there before that happens."

Everyone realised it was essential to hurry, and the oozies urged the elephants into a faster pace—on occasions like this none of the Burmans ever got panicky, as they had great faith in Jim and always seemed to feel he could manage any situation which might arise.

We pressed on and in an hour's time reached the river. It was a relief to all of us to find that although it was muddy and angry looking, it was still only ankle deep.

"These streams can rise at least twelve feet in under an hour," said Jim, "and we had better get Treve and Naw Lah across first as quickly as we can."

Even as we watched, the water was flowing faster and getting deeper, and branches and other flotsam were starting to come down—a sure sign that a rise was imminent. Poor little Naw Lah looked like a drowned rat—her sleek black hair was soaking wet and her bright cotton skirt clung sodden and uncomfortable round her small figure. She knew the danger of crossing the river at this moment, but didn't hesitate for a second. Her only thought was for Treve and even now she made him laugh under his improvised tent as they waded in.

Jim had hung back a moment or two to make sure the elephants were following, and seeing Treve was safely across, I waited for him. By the time we reached mid-stream, we were both up to our waists in swirling murky water—the force of it was frightening. I had a long stick with me and dug it hard into the stream bed; but even so, if Jim had not held his stave so that I could hang on to it, I should have been swept off my feet.

We struggled up the other side—wet, cold, and bedraggled—and sat waiting anxiously for the elephants. They were only just in the nick of time. As they crossed, the river had already risen up to the level of the baggage on their backs. They could have swum had they been unloaded, but if they had done so now we should have lost all our things.

Fortunately there was a Forest Rest House not far away, and we were glad to stay the night there and dry out our clothes. This abnormal rainfall had made me realise in a small way what travel in the jungle must be like in the rainy season, and I knew now why it was we were not allowed to tour with our husbands then.

That evening I had the tremendous thrill of seeing for the first time a rise bringing logs down the river with it. This usually happened about the middle of May, and it was then that the worries of the forest men really started.

Jim told me they would wait anxiously for the first heavy downpour of rain, and that it was almost possible to smell it approaching. First they would see wisps of cloud being chased across the sky by the hot wind, which rustled through the trees and gradually lowered the stifling temperature. Then came the huge black mass of cumulus and the first heavy drops of rain, followed by flashes of lightning and great crashes of thunder—the monsoon had arrived.

The dust became squelching mud and the water cascaded from the trees and from the thatch of the jungle huts. In contrast to the previous heat, there would be a cold wet chill to strike at the body. Insects of every shape, size and smell emerged from everywhere to sing their welcome to the pouring rain.

They attacked in their millions, varying from sandflies of almost pinpoint size up through the range of mosquitoes and stink bugs, whose smell defies description, to the very large dung beetle. The bull frogs distended their throats and hurled out their croakings, and the cicadas increased the shrill tempo of their never-ending cries.

The sight of the first rise of the year coming down a stream bed could be terrifying. A wall of water, sometimes six feet deep, would hurl itself along, carrying all before it—boulders and sand tossed into the air by the onrush of the churned-up racing floods. Great teak logs, which minutes previously had lain on the dry sand looking solidly immovable, some of them weighing eight tons or even more, were picked up and swirled around like matchsticks in a mill race.

The noise was deafening. Above the hissing and gurgling of the racing torrents rose the boom boom as the logs crashed together in the fury of the spate—hundreds of them being hurled along, their butt ends pointing skywards, then sinking again like vast overgrown porpoises.

As soon as he heard this first rise, it was the job of the forest man to get his elephants distributed to the various bends in the river where he knew the logs would probably be washed up on the bank. The task of these elephants was to get the logs back into the stream and to keep them moving on their way to the saw mill: a journey which might take seven or eight years.

Often the job was complicated by logs getting jammed and forming themselves into vast stockades of interlocked timber. This jamming usually occurred in the first rises of the season, as the water then came down with such force that it caused the logs to bounce. One or two would sink butt down into soft sand and, before they had time to clear themselves, others soon formed round them. In no time there was a jam involving hundreds of logs, and if these were not freed with the utmost speed, it would mean the channel being blocked for weeks.

One of the most wonderful sights to watch was an experienced elephant going into the racing water to break up a jam. It was an extremely dangerous job both for the great animal and for the oozie on his head.

Knowing his job and his elephant, he would not urge it on too much, but allow the animal to make sure of its footholds and make its own way steadily forward. The elephant always kept a weather eye upstream to ensure that he would not be knocked down by timber racing from above. Slowly, steadily, he would make his way out to the jam, trunk held high away from the water swirling round his flanks.

An experienced animal would instinctively select the key log. Placing one of his forefeet on it, he would gently rock it until there was a creaking sound of movement and the jam would start to break up. Then the elephant would back his way to the bank, always with his eye upstream; he would never turn round and walk out, for in doing so he would have left himself unguarded, and this could have meant the difference between survival and disaster.

*   *   *

That night Jim and I talked together about monsoons and rises, and some of the experiences he had had of them in the past. He told me a story about a rise that two tusker elephants of his had once had to deal with. He always told a story well and this one was so graphic and in such detail that I shall never forget the impression it made on me. I often heard it again in later years, for he frequently included it in his lectures to illustrate the elephant's intelligence. Here it is.

It was the month of May and sweltering hot. The prayer of all living things was that God would soon send his rain and monsoons to spring-clean the forest streams and bring forth green fodder again.

Some engineers of the Public Works Department wished otherwise, for they had but three weeks, before the break of the monsoon, to finish a light railway bridge over the Wuntho River.

Jim had seen the bridge in course of construction and wondered how the two large timber piers would stand up to the strain of floating teak logs when the first large spate arrived. Eight miles above the bridge he had some 2,800 logs lying in the bed of the river. It was a dry sandy bed and he knew full well that when the first spate arrived they would be away.

The logs had been strung out with the smallest downstream, increasing in size as they were laid out upstream; the intention being that the small logs would float away first.

His work was completed but the engineers' was not, for they knew they could not batten the piers before the break of the monsoon; that is, trim them on the upstream side shaped as the bows of a ship, so as to divert floating logs through the three archways, a centre one and one to each bank.

They went to Jim with their troubles, asking if he would remove all logs from the river bed for that season. He refused, for it was too late in the year to use elephants in such a scorched area, where there was no fodder for them.

They then took to paper, and sent Jim official letters, informing him that he would be responsible for any damage done, explaining that damage would mean destruction which could not be permitted at any cost. Jim again refused, and they took it to higher authority, and obtained an order to him from some big-wig in Rangoon.

In a fury, Jim destroyed the order, packed up fishing tackle, and went on tour to the headwaters of the Nanpo River, quite near the Wuntho, where there was fast running water. There he could at least think it over—catch a mahseer and inspect elephants camped on the banks.

In these camps were two tusker elephants named Poo Chang and Poo Gyi. "Lane bah thees," the elephant men called them, meaning "wise old animals".

Watching one of them standing in fast flowing water one evening gave Jim an idea for an experiment. He would train them both for a short period whilst camped there, floating logs down at them, using them as imaginary piers, and see if they would react by passing the logs right and left with their massive heads and tusks, as if diverting them through the archways of the bridge. For he was determined not to carry out the order to remove the 2,800 logs from the river bed of the Wuntho.

At dawn the following day he explained to Poo Chang's and Poo Gyi's respective oozies what he wished to do, and they placed both tuskers abreast against the current, at a distance apart equal to that between the two piers of the bridge.

The oozies were amused, and expressed opinions that no practice was necessary, but Jim warned them that maybe it would be dangerous when the time came, in flood water of the Wuntho River.

From above the position of the two animals standing in the Nanpo, Jim employed a camp of ten elephants to launch logs into the fast current. It was as if the elephants understood exactly, for as the logs came towards their respective heads the oozie merely shouted "Coming right", "Coming left", and as they came they were diverted by their tusks to right and left.

When he was fully satisfied that the two elephants understood perfectly what they had to do, he trained another pair, Po Sein and Po Sih, as reliefs; thus making a team of four.

He was so encouraged that he replied again to the order, saying that it was impossible to carry it out, because of the expected early break of the monsoons, but that he would endeavour to protect the bridge.

With the first thunderstorms and rain, when the heat had so stoked up in the heavens that it seemed as if something just had to happen soon, be it torrential tropical rain or an earthquake, Jim moved camp to the bridge, taking Poo Chang, Poo Gyi, and the relief pair. There was only a trickle of water passing below the bridge. It was deserted and appeared naked above the logs, as if the fires of the hot season or the waters of the monsoon would eventually claim it.

How Jim loathed that bridge—for he had to camp by it until the rains came, and only those who knew what an aching body that could cause could appreciate it. The grumbling thunder in the distant hills, the inky-black build-up of clouds raised hopes, only to disappoint within an hour.

He waited two whole weeks. It seemed as if the very boles of the giant trees around would soon crack under the merciless sun, and mature bamboos were actually doing so. Everything he could do had been done: his fire-watchers on the 2,800 logs eight miles above had been ordered to send him warning as soon as there was any sign of a cloud-burst in the headwaters, or as soon as the water changed colour, or any indications of a full spate. He prayed for a full spate if it came at all.

It occurred at night. The heavens seemed to split, rain was torrential. Lightning seemed to travel down the bare boles of tree trunks, to pass along the game tracks and sizzle out like fire in the sheet of rain. Thunder followed in such cracks instead of rumbles that everything shook. The monsoon had broken, not only against the hills and mountains, but was tearing across the forests of Burma by night. Every living thing in the jungles had waited for this, knowing it would arrive as some terrifying monster. A howling cyclone wind came with it, driving the rain into every corner to clean up the jungle.

Now that it had come it was exciting. Jim's servants came to say that the river would rise. His head elephant man came to say Poo Chang and Poo Gyi were ready, tethered to two solitary trees. Flashes of lightning lit up the bare bridge like some ghostly skeleton, to leave pitch darkness again and utter loss of recollection as to its position.

His head elephant man became uneasy. Their hopes were fading—the spate would deliver the logs against the bridge in the dark instead of in daylight. The *nats* would decide that before dawn. Hopes grew as the hours passed towards dawn, yet there was no break in this torrential downpour.

With the first signs of light a young Burman arrived from the log camp with a message to expect flood water that day. The sandy river bed had soaked up the first deluge like a sponge— little rivulets were forming, flowing towards the winding channel. Water was changing colour. A small tributary near camp belched forth a mass of leaves and debris, which seemed to be a signal for the same thing happening to thousands of similar ones away in the mountainous headwaters of this Wuntho catchment area.

A sheet of water appeared a mile above Jim's camp—it was like quicksilver covering small yellow sun-baked sandbanks, now disappearing like magic. Water was taking the place of sand. One wave of it came like a small bore, and the sandy river bed was soon a sheet of brown muddy water.

There was no excitement or panic amongst the elephant men, for they knew that the first sign would be a dug-out canoe coming down stream to say logs were actually moving.

Jim sat with his head elephant man in the portico of his tent. The storm break had passed, but it was still raining heavily. It seemed as if the whole three hundred inches for the season would fall in one day.

There was suddenly a cheer from camp. The headman jumped up, saying, "He's coming, Thakin—see him?" Round the bend from up-stream Jim saw two small figures in a dug-out canoe, paddling for all they were worth, helped by the current of water, now rising steadily.

The two oozies of Poo Chang and Poo Gyi came to his tent, excited, asking if they should not man their elephants and get into position in front of the piers, for leaves and small debris were already building up. They were told it would be an hour yet—maybe two, maybe three—before any logs came down, and to go and have some rice for the last time of the day before evening. They did as they were told, but that

'I was in it up to my ears'

In the logging camp

Treating a crushed toenail

they were excited pleased Jim, for then the Burman is at his best.

A group of men from the camp met the dug-out canoe. It pulled in to the bank alongside the camp site, about one hundred yards above the bridge where the bank was high. They shouted to Jim, "Hurry, for the logs are coming—the whole watershed is in spate."

This was enough for the two oozies to act immediately, and they disappeared to the jungle for Poo Chang and Poo Gyi.

Jim was now so worked up that he felt they would never appear, but at last they did, riding their respective animals in a slow walk, as if tomorrow would do. That was the attitude of the elephants it seemed, for they were enjoying the cool rain, and this was a new world. The rains had broken and everything was saturated instead of being scorched.

Jim thought those elephants would never get into position. They were rather hesitant in moving into the river, for no timber elephant likes to be moved from camp and separated during floods—they like company.

A few odd branches of trees had passed the camp and gone under the bridge—drawn actually by the current passing through the archways—but one had caught in the pier, and as Poo Gyi arrived at his station at the far pier his oozie directed him to release it, and away it went.

Both animals had now taken up positions facing up-current. Water was lapping their under-bellies. The oozies were all smiles, their bare shoulders looking cool and shining in the downpour of rain—their oily long hair tied pony-tail fashion on their necks. Each carried a small short cane, and they had taken their bearings on how to jump onto their respective piers in case things got out of hand.

There was another loud cheer from the camp men, who were now lining the bank, and two or three excited youngsters shouted "Yauk byee! Thit lone yauk byee!" (Logs have arrived.)

All eyes were directed up river—yes, they were coming in batches of three or four together, as if there were some static attraction for them to remain in touch with each other. Some came singly. The small ones twisting and turning in the ever-changing current—they were scattering. Every now and then a log would ground and hold up on a shallow submerged sand-bank, as if making an effort to remain in the forest where for a century its parent tree had taken that time or more to grow. But the rising water would eat the sandbank away, and on it came—the first movement of logs by water for the fifteen hundred miles they had to go for conversion into timber.

Poo Chang was the nearest animal to where Jim stood watching. He was tempted to stand on the bridge, but had given orders that no one was to watch from there for fear of disturbing the elephants.

There was a cheer and laughter as Poo Chang jabbed his tusks at the first arrival of a log. He just sent it spinning to his off side, to be drawn into the current and away under the bridge. Another to his off side, then three consecutive ones to his near side. Poo Gyi was protecting his pier in the same efficient manner. All small logs were passing like skittles or corks, each one appearing as if it aimed at piling up against the elephants as obstructions. The elephants in turn giving them a determined jab to prevent it.

The pace soon became furious and the elephants' heads were swinging right and left with scarcely a miss, diverting the logs with grace and ease. Occasionally a log would glance off the belly of an elephant, but Jim did not see one get through the guard without being jabbed by tusks, as if to say, "Get on with you!"

The pace then slackened. Well over five hundred small logs had passed. Then came the logs of greater length and girth, and these were the most dangerous, for if one happened to strand across from pier to pier, or against a pile, others would soon stock up. The water was still rising, and the movement of the elephants made it clear that they were feeling the scour around their feet in the sand, but no one knew better than the elephant how to correct that, for it came by instinct.

Long heavy logs came silently down in the current, occasionally swinging around in the eddies. It was as if the elephants took a sight along their outstretched trunks on these logs as they approached like crocodiles. With the impetus of the current and a weight of three to four tons behind some of them, Poo Chang would draw himself up as if to meet them. Instead of jabbing, he used his power increasingly, steering the log away from him and following it through to disappear under the archway, and on.

Jim hesitated whether to change the animals, or to add two more as it was obvious that Poo Chang and Poo Gyi were tiring, but he feared disturbance and congestion. The heavy butt logs of eight to ten feet in girth, but only sixteen or seventeen feet long were just arriving. They were at well-spaced intervals. Many of them were grounding for periods on end, but the water was still rising and on they came. They floated heavily, two-thirds below water, one-third above, and many of them were five to six tons in weight. The danger of logs piling up against the piers had passed, but logs of this description striking the piers would have shaken them to their base, and Jim prayed that the elephants would stand, or that the flood spate had reached its maximum height.

There was a sudden shout from the camp men and a fresh bore of water arrived, releasing many of the grounded big-girth logs. Poo Chang was now almost afloat and each time he handled a big log now, he ducked his head under water, nearly unseating his rider.

There was a long pause before the arrival of the next log. Jim suddenly saw the oozie stand on Poo Chang's head and then run up his bare back and clamber on to a ledge on the pier above the animal. Poo Chang's reaction was immediate, for he swung half round as if to say "I am off, too," to swim away in the current through the archway and under the bridge, but his oozie checked him. He yelled the words "Poo

Chang!" in time, with a meaning of "You dare swim away and funk it!"

Poo Chang turned back again to face the current and an enormous on-coming log. In his anger, he dealt it a blow which submerged it and on it went; then another followed and obeying word-of-mouth orders from his oozie, now on the pier, the animal still stood his ground. Poo Gyi was getting none of this excitement. It was at fever pitch, and Jim rather hoped that Poo Chang would desert his post, for little damage could be done now except by pure misfortune, for logs were few and far between.

Poo Chang perhaps guessed Jim's feelings, for he did swing right round as if to swim away, but again the oozie shrieked, "Poo Chang! Poo Chang!" Again he obeyed, but this time he was right around. Then he plunged his forefeet securely into the sandy bed of the river. The fast-racing current passed over his hindquarters, now facing up-stream. He half turned his head, with a glance as if to say, "Watch this log kick my bottom." They all watched—it was enormous. It was coming end on, but as it struck him he wagged his big stern like a porpoise and glanced it off with an ease which drew cheers from all who watched.

He repeated it again and again, warned each time by his oozie from above him, and as each log was dealt a boomps-a-daisy, the camp men cheered.

He remained at his post in this attitude for another hour, and then Jim relieved Poo Chang and Poo Gyi with Po Sein and Po Sin. Soon it became evident that single stranded logs remained stranded. The water was falling, and it continued to do so until sundown.

It was a triumph for the elephants—not one log damaged a pier. I think, too, it was a triumph for Jim.

CHAPTER XXIII

THE MOST INTELLIGENT ANIMAL

THERE was one elephant, called Bandoola, who was of very special interest to Jim, as he was one of the first, under the new plan, that had been reared in captivity from a small calf and trained up to be a working elephant. Because he was such a magnificent animal he had been named Bandoola, after a famous Burmese general, and his whole career had been closely followed for the last thirty-eight years, ever since he was born. It was an expensive education too, to rear these elephants, for by the time they were twenty-one years of age, and fully developed physically and mentally, it had cost roughly twelve hundred pounds. Had an adult kheddared animal been bought, the price would have been about the same, but there was no comparison in appearance or intelligence.

By the time he was twenty-one years old and ready to go to work, Bandoola almost knew the Burmese language. He was now working dragging timber near a logging camp which lay on our route.

Jim had told Treve endless stories about Bandoola—the elephant was used as a sort of symbol of determination which had thoroughly caught his imagination. Treve would often say, when faced with some difficulty, "Well, could Bandoola do it?" And on being told, "Yes, he would have a good try"—would make the effort himself.

So he too was filled with excitement when he saw his hero elephant standing before him for the first time. "Show me what he can do," he said to Po Toke, his oozie.

Po Toke was only too glad to show off Bandoola's prowess—
he was his hero, too. He laid down ten articles in front of him
—an axe, a saw, three different sizes of chains, a hammer, etc.

"Give me the saw," he said in Burmese.

Bandoola looked along the row of implements and immediately passed up the saw, with his trunk, to Po Toke.

"All right, put it down," he said. "Now pass me the
hammer." This too was picked out without a moment's
hesitation; and then the rest of the articles were passed up in
turn without a mistake.

"You're a fine big gentleman," said Po Toke, and Bandoola
seemed to take it as the compliment it was meant to be.

Po Toke then climbed down from the elephant's head, took
up one end of a chain in his hands and told Bandoola to tie
it in a knot. This he did with great vigour, twisting it with
his trunk into a knot that no human hand would have had the
strength to untie. However, when Bandoola was told to loosen
it, he did so as if it were a piece of string. Treve was delighted.

"Oh, he can do more than that," said Po Toke with pride.
"You come and watch what he can do with a tree."

He rode him a few paces to where some young trees were
growing. This time all the orders were carried out without a
word of command—there was no saddle, no whip—just the
pressure of the inner thigh against the animal's neck, and a
touch of the oozie's big toe behind his ear.

Each time, Po Toke indicated to us what he was going to ask
Bandoola to do, then silently conveyed his wishes to the animal,
whose powers of differentiation were quite remarkable. We
saw him respond to a series of unspoken instructions. Turn
left—turn right—put his head back—put his head down—pull
a branch down—push a tree down—pull up a sapling, or
simply protect a sapling.

There have been many arguments about the intelligence of
elephants; but this demonstration, and all the other exhibitions
of their cleverness that I had seen in the jungle, convinced me
that Jim's theory that the elephant is the most intelligent

animal in the world was true. I have heard people say that it is not so much intelligence as obedience and habit; but I think it is the animal's combination of intelligence and obedience which is unique.

His intelligence does not drive him to take matters into his own hands and do what he thinks best; but he can be relied upon to obey with great patience the orders of his riders, even going so far as to swallow unpleasant medicine. Even more remarkable, he will submit himself to the painful removal of ulcers and to other surgery by those whom he really trusts— seeming always to understand that it is all for his own good.

As the elephant's obedience is largely the result of affection, his training has to be done with great gentleness and kindness —in any case, it would hardly be possible to use force on such a powerful animal.

So far as habit is concerned, all Jim's observations had led him to believe that an elephant is in fact very tractable and adaptable. For instance, he will settle down quite happily if his occupation is changed, or his hours altered, or even when, for some reason, he has to be taken over by a new oozie.

When an elephant is given some task to do, his obedience makes him continue almost without supervision until it is completed; and the fact that he has this power of concentration makes some people feel that he should be able to go on without further instruction. Instead of which, if the oozie is not looking, he will give himself the luxury of strolling off to feed, or to have a dust bath, when the immediate task is done.

However, Jim had a story which shows that this is not always the case. Two men were sawing a log, and one of them wanted to go off and have a sleep, so he gave his end of the saw over to the elephant, and told him to carry on. After a bit, his partner got sleepy too, and left the elephant sawing alone, which he continued to do all by himself until the job was finished. Somebody at the mills was so intrigued by this that he took a photograph, a copy of which was given to Jim.

Just as we were about to go, Treve turned to Jim. "I could

do everything Bandoola does," he said. "But I don't know about the tree part," he added, rather doubtfully.

"Never mind," said Jim, "he's much older than you. He's as old as I am—exactly the same age, in fact, and we both started working in the jungle at the same time, too."

It was time to go, and when we said goodbye, Po Toke gave us one last recital of his elephant's remarkable qualities. Neither he nor we knew then that in a few years' time these same qualities would be the means of Bandoola saving the lives of just on two hundred people.

Treve's love of animals sometimes caused difficulties on the march. A few days later, we were trekking down one of the inevitable ridges towards the creek below. Naw Lah and Treve were a little ahead when she gave a scream—as she walked along she had disturbed a huge iguana or 'put'; it was about three feet long, and looked rather like a small alligator.

It tore away over the dry leaves, making as much noise as a bison breaking cover, bolted down the hillside, and disappeared among the large rocks. Treve shrieked with excitement, and begged to be allowed to run ahead after it. Naw Lah would not hear of such a thing, but we all followed as quickly as possible and began to hunt under the boulders and in any likely holes.

Jim always seemed to have a sixth sense about the habits of any animal and knew exactly where to look. He went straight to a large pool and pointed to where the iguana was lying absolutely still on some small pebbles in about three feet of water. Its colours blended perfectly with its surroundings, and even when we were quite close it was difficult to make it out; its foundation colour of mustard yellow with upper markings of black circular rings gave it complete camouflage.

The Burmans with us were quite excited too, as they love to eat the 'put's' eggs which it deposits in a hole in the sand—several of them sometimes lay in one nest, and we have come across as many as ten dozen eggs altogether in the same burrow. But above all, its flesh is a great delicacy, and is said to taste like chicken. So Aung Net did not hesitate with this one; he pulled off his headdress, wound it round his hand and forearm to protect himself from the creature's jaws, then plunged his arm into the pool and grabbed it.

Jim was about to kill it, as Aung Net, being a Buddhist, would not do so—believing in reincarnation, he might inadvertently be killing cousin Ma Hla or Uncle Maung San; he looked forward to eating the creature, as long as the actual deed was done by someone else.

But Treve had different ideas; for some reason, he had taken a tremendous liking to this unattractive-looking creature, and was most upset at the thought that it was about to die.

"It can ride along with me," he said. "Do let me keep it."

We laughed. "It wouldn't make too bad a pet, either," said Jim, "except for those awful claws—bigger and sharper than an eagle's!" However, to please Treve we put it in a slatted crate and promised that, for the time being anyway, it would not be killed.

Towards evening, Jim and I went to look at it. Neither of us could bear the sight of it caged up like this, so we decided to let it go, and to tell Treve in the morning that we had had to do so for its own good. Jim called Aung Net and told him we were not going to keep it any longer, so would he take it away and release it in the forest.

Later that night we were sitting by the fire when we heard Joseph call across to the others, "Come on, chaps, I have made some 'put' curry for supper tonight."

"Blighters," said Jim, "they've killed it to eat, after all. They must have got Joseph to do it—he's the only one who isn't a Buddhist."

Aung Net told us afterwards that it had never entered their heads that once we had finished with it we would object to their eating it.

Next morning we told Treve exactly what had happened. Jim always felt, and rightly so I think, that whenever possible a child should not have the true facts hidden from it, but as it grows up it should always be given a picture of life as it really is—a mixture of unexpected joys and griefs, intermingled with mistakes and disappointments which have to be taken as part of the whole.

He took it well, and Naw Lah was obviously very much relieved. "I am glad to see the last of it," she said; although, being a Karen, she probably thought a good deal more than she gave voice to.

All in all, she had stood up to these tours remarkably well, and soon came really to enjoy them, at any rate in the daytime; at night, though, her innate fear of the jungle sometimes overcame her. It was not until years afterwards that she admitted to me how she would sometimes lie awake wondering what animals were prowling near our tents, and when she heard the trumpeting of wild elephants, not far away, she had wondered why she had ever agreed to come with us.

We were both very upset that she, who had such a game spirit, should have been unlucky enough to have a bout of malaria on this trip. I myself had had it several times, and once, just before Treve was born, had been seriously ill with it, so I knew the signs well.

Poor Naw Lah started to shiver and shake all over. I piled every available blanket on top of her, but even in this climate her teeth were chattering with the cold chill, the initial onslaught of this disease. Her temperature then started to rise, and quickly soared to 105 degrees.

The fever persisted all day, and her constant cry was, "I want to go home, I want to go home!"

I tried to comfort her by telling her that as soon as she was better we would make arrangements for her to do so. We were really worried, but fortunately after heavy doses of quinine the fever broke, and after sweating profusely for an hour or two, she began to feel better.

We stayed where we were for some days while she regained her strength, and were then able to put her on Jim's pony, Nicky, for the next move. In an incredibly short time she became her usual cheerful self, and the thought of going home never entered her head again.

Looking back on these attacks of malaria, it always amazes me how, after being seriously ill with really high temperatures, one was able to get up and about again in so short a time. When Jim was younger, he always used to know about an hour before when an attack was about to come on. He would go to bed, be down with high fever for a couple of hours, sweat it out, then manage to carry on as usual.

Sometimes this would happen as often as every other day; those who were strong were able to stand the ever-recurring bouts that the young Assistant had to endure, but over the years it took its toll of those of weaker physique. As a result, a large number of them developed blackwater fever, which was usually fatal.

CHAPTER XXIV

WAR COMES TO THE EAST

WHEN we arrived home three months later, the hot weather was on us again; in this place the temperature often touched well over 110 degrees in the shade. Jim and I had stayed through it for one season, but it had been an exhausting experience which we did not want Treve to have to go through. We were due for leave in England, but owing to the war this could not be, so we decided to go up to Maymyo instead.

Maymyo was a township lying on the slopes of the Shan hills, fifty-six miles north of Mandalay, and we could not have picked a lovelier place; although only a hundred miles from Shwebo, we might have been on a different planet. To be lifted from the airless plain into the soft breezes and cool air of the hills breathed new life into us all.

As we climbed the perilous hairpin road from Mandalay we began to feel revived by the bracing air; colour flowed into Treve's cheeks, and the dogs were at last able to close their mouths in contentment and stop panting.

When we saw the house that we had taken for the next six months, standing among cherry trees in full bloom, the war seemed further away than ever. This was an easy life amongst rolling lawns and magnificent trees. The nights were cool and the days pleasantly warm; there were strawberry teas, and servants to wait on us—everything about it lulled one out of reality—even the jungle was forgotten for the time being.

The teak companies had made a little oasis up here, where

their men on leave, whose lives for the greater part of the year were uncomfortable, rigorous and isolated, could relax.

It was a tremendous contrast for me too, and to be able to wear a pretty dress without being soaked with sweat in less than half an hour was in itself a luxury. Jim was never happy idling for long, but the lazy existence by day and the ceaseless parties at night, were a relaxation for us both.

But life does not allow one to dream for too long, and while we had been enjoying ourselves here in Maymyo a great tragedy had befallen Jim's brother Tom, who was a mining engineer working in India. One day a telegram arrived telling us that his wife had suddenly died. She had left a small girl aged two and a half and a boy of six months, and we were most worried as to how he would be able to cope.

We cabled straight away offering to have them here with us. But Tom was overcome with grief and could not bring himself to part with them. He tried gallantly to struggle on looking after them himself for five months and then realised that he ought to accept our offer for the children's sake.

He brought them to us in Maymyo in the early spring. Diana, the little girl, had been deeply upset. In addition, she had had dysentery and was far from well. Michael, the baby, was bouncing and fit, his father having looked after him wonderfully, carrying on exactly as before his wife died. But he was eleven months old now, and needed more solid food than the bottles which he had been having.

Tom had to return to India in three weeks' time, but we had made arrangements that he would have the children again for the cold weather months.

My heart bled for poor little Diana; although she was now only three, she felt the loss to the depths of her being, and from the moment she had come to us had not let Tom out of her sight. After he had gone, it was several weeks before she had any feeling of security.

In the end it was Treve who won her over and made her feel 'belonged'. To Jim and me, they really became part of our family, and we quickly grew to love them both as much as we did our own son. He too benefited enormously from their company, and all three children looked completely different after a month or two in the hills.

*   *   *

We were not looking forward to returning to Shwebo. We had nearly completed seven years there, which was an unusually long time to be in any station, and we were very much hoping that our new posting, when it came, would be somewhere healthier for the children.

This time luck was with us, or it may have been simply that the company felt that after so many years in unpleasant climates, we deserved a respite: to our joy we heard that Jim had been given the Shweli Forest for his new area, with his headquarters here in Maymyo. Nothing could have pleased us more; this would be a real home for the children, and very much like they would have had in England.

Labour was cheap in those days, and there was no lack of help. Not only did I have Naw Lah to look after Treve, but two other Karen girls, one for Diana and the other for Michael. There was someone to do the cooking, several to do the cleaning, two or three to do the waiting—and even a boy especially to look after the dogs.

What extraordinary contrasts life in those days presented to people living and working in Burma, as we did. There were luxuries such as we had here in Maymyo, which we shall never experience again; then, for a great part of the time, there were conditions of such discomfort in the jungle that I find it difficult to believe I ever went through them. But then it all seemed to fall into one pattern, and being young and belonging to that era, I accepted both parts of the life with equal lack of questioning.

For Jim, the hard life had far outweighed the times of ease. He also saw farther and deeper into the whole picture than any of us wives did, and more so than most of the men who worked with him. A great many of these took their privileges as a matter of course, although it must be said that they also faced up to their hardships with the same spirit.

Our life of ease here in Maymyo lasted for a year, and we enjoyed it to the full. To the British, living here in their pipe dream, war clouds seemed far away. The war was brought home to us a little when a Bush Warfare School was established nearby, and we met many British soldiers who had come on here from war service in Greece, and who were already worn and weary. To them, we must have seemed a casual crowd with no thought for the future, as we arranged and rearranged our gardens and planned for the years that never were.

In November, 1941, Diana and Michael flew back to India for a visit to their father, and Treve and I set off with Jim for what was to be our last jungle tour. Going off from here meant a journey to Mandalay by road, then a day's journey by rail north from Mandalay to Katha, which lay at the junction of the Shweli and Irrawaddy rivers.

From there we had a small launch at our disposal, and it took us another two days up-river before we reached jungle headquarters where we met up with our elephants and struck off into the forest. How peaceful it was—camped under the huge trees in a world of sunlight and shadow; it did not seem possible that war could affect us.

Then the bombshell came. We heard on the wireless that the Japs had attacked Pearl Harbour and a few days later the unbelievable news of the sinking of *The Prince of Wales* and *The Repulse*. The East was now involved in the war. I don't think even then I realised how serious this was going to be for us and Jim did not pass on how worried he was feeling and we both tried to enter into the spirit of Christmas when it came a few weeks later.

In the years gone by, when we had been on our own, we had never felt very much like celebrating Christmas Day in the jungle and it was very much one of routine work; but now that Treve was with us we decorated our little temporary jungle hut, and Jim cut down a branch to improvise a Christmas tree. Naw Lah festooned this most beautifully with anything she could find to hand—being a Christian, she was determined to make the very most of the day for Treve.

Early in January, 1942, a runner arrived in camp with the mail, and among the letters was an urgent telegram telling us to return to Mandalay immediately.

With my head still in the clouds I remember saying to Jim, "Can't we pretend we never received it and go on with our tour?"

But Jim of course realised how serious it was. "You must remember," he said, "that we are far from everywhere. This telegram has been on the way for over a week—for all we know, the Japs may be in Rangoon already. We must pack up and leave immediately." This was the moment when I was shaken into reality.

The elephant men and jungle Burmans couldn't understand it at all. "If there is any danger you would be far safer to stay with us here in the jungle," they said.

We hated leaving them like this, and told them we should be back as soon as possible—and we both thought we would. Mirzah Khan, our night-watchman from Shwebo, who was now in charge of the ponies, came to say goodbye to Treve. He was the only one among the men who seemed to sense what was really happening, and with tears streaming down his face he said, "I shall never see the Baba again."

I shall always remember how Treve, seeing his grief, turned to me with a puzzled look, saying, "Why does he love me so much, Mummy?"

The journey out, which we had made so recently with such leisure and enjoyment, now became a frantic rush in the opposite direction. The next two days we marched without rest before joining the launch again down-river.

Five days later we arrived in Mandalay and were met by a Forest Manager who told us that things were going badly; the Japanese advance into Burma had already begun, and

'What mother does I can do too'

A downy baby has finished its bath

Laying the foundations for a bridge in wartime

The rains have come

there had been several bombing raids on Rangoon. Although we were hundreds of miles from the scene of action, it was feared that Burma might be invaded, and the Bombay Burmah Corporation had decided to evacuate the women and children of their personnel.

We were to go by train and launch to Mawlaik. Once there, the company felt that if the worst happened we could at least march out, with the aid of elephants, to the railhead in Manipur, and from there we should be able to get away by train to India, and safety.

It all sounded most unlikely. As for marching the hundred and seventy miles from Mawlaik to Manipur—it never entered my head that such a thing would ever become necessary. My only thought for the moment was to get back home to Maymyo and have a rest and collect my things together.

I told the man in charge that that was what I wanted to do. He looked at me rather pityingly. "This is an emergency," he said. "You're late already—all the other wives and children have left their homes and gone."

Jim backed me up. I was expecting another baby and had a desperate yearning to go home, even if only for one night, and he managed to persuade the Forest Manager to let us go, promising that we would be back next day, saying that one day more or less could not matter.

It was a joy to return to our house. I always felt this way when I got back from the jungle, after living in tents—everything was so spotless and orderly. Treve rushed to his toys—all new and exciting again after weeks of absence from them. It would be hard to explain that we had to leave it all; but that night, with the long journey behind us, and the uncertainty ahead, we were very tired and sank into our comfortable beds and slept well.

At the back of my mind I felt that the Japs would be held and that we should be returning soon. So much so— and perhaps, in a way, to reassure myself—that I packed nothing much; a small suitcase for myself and one for

Treve—just simple needs, such as we usually took on a jungle tour.

Jim hardly took anything—only a grip with a change of shirt and his night things. His plan was to accompany us on the first part of the rail journey as far as Monywa, where we were to board a launch up the Chindwin. As I was expecting a baby I was feeling none too good, and he was worried about the crowds of refugees whom we heard were piling onto the trains.

We stepped out of our house the following morning taking Naw Lah, Aung Net, Joseph and a young Burman called San Pyu with us. All our belongings including the ponies, dogs, cats, pigeons, and Treve's guinea pigs, were left behind. We little knew that we should never see any of them again.

CHAPTER XXV

THE EXODUS BEGINS

W HEN we got to Monywa we found that the second party of women and children, who had gone ahead of us, had not yet left on the next stage of their journey up the Chindwin. They had all come without their menfolk, and when the Bombay Burmah man in charge here saw Jim accompanying me, it immediately solved a problem for him.

"We were getting desperate," he said, "trying to find some-one responsible to take all these women and children to Mawlaik."

But Jim thought otherwise. "I just can't," he said. "I have left my men in the jungle, promising that I would come back and pay them, and I couldn't let them down. Also, all our animals are left at home in Maymyo—I must get back."

However, he was persuaded to wait while a telegram was sent to Rangoon for instructions. The answer came back that he was to escort us as far as Mawlaik and then await further orders.

The party of about fifty boarded the little launch that had carried us to Mawlaik on this very same journey up river when we were first married. As we went down the gang plank I thought of dear Molly, and the job we had had to make her go across it; there had only been three passengers on that occasion, but now there were over fifty.

The boat was built to take six people with comfort, so we were packed very tightly together, and arrangements for washing and feeding were difficult. At night we fitted ourselves in to sleep as best we could—on deck, or anywhere that a space could be found. I was glad that Naw Lah was with us, for as usual she was unperturbed and kept Treve happy.

As we steamed along up river another little boat followed in our wake. In it we were towing a mother and her three children, one of whom had developed measles; Jim had isolated them like this to prevent all the rest from catching it.

Once in Mawlaik, general depression set in; no one knew how long we would have to wait here in these very over-crowded conditions while events settled themselves. I was lucky, for I had Jim with me. Most of the wives, whose husbands were on tour when the order came to move away, had no idea when they would see them again, or how they were going to get out if Burma should fall.

There was now general disruption in the country. Mails soon became non-existent; the only communication was with Rangoon, and that was by wire alone. Everyone was worried above all about what would happen to the homes left behind. Jim kept my spirits up. He was still hoping to go back to see to things and to retrieve the animals, even if Treve and I were not able to return.

In the meantime, he had had instructions that he and the other company personnel here in Mawlaik were to get busy making arrangements in case we had to make the long march out of the country. Tinned foods were checked and sorted. Orders were given that all work in the forests was to cease, so that as many elephants as possible could be mustered together in readiness. These were not to be used for carrying people, but only for stores and tents and personal belongings.

Canvas hammocks were made so that they could be slung between two poles in order to carry the children who were too young to walk, and Chin coolies were hired as carriers and told to stand by. At the moment, all the children were quite happy, and a lot of those who had come from out-of-the-way places were thrilled to have so many companions to play with.

In spite of the preparations, we women went on talking as

though we thought everything was only a temporary measure, and continued to make plans for the return to our homes.

Jim's hopes of returning were soon knocked on the head when a message came through giving instructions that, if the march out had to be made, Geoff Bostock, a Forest Inspector and an old friend of Jim's, was to be in charge of the women and children, and Jim was to go too, and organise the elephants. Mrs. Bostock and I were allotted the task of planning and arranging for all meals en route. I was very glad I would be working with her as I knew what a capable and efficient person she was. Joseph was detailed to be one of the cooks for the party.

Our spirits ebbed to zero when, after we had been in Mawlaik about a fortnight, news came through that Singapore had fallen to the Japanese and that we must start moving.

What a cavalcade it was that set off on that February morning. There were about twenty women and fifteen children in our party, some of them small babies. Most of these families had never been to the jungle before, and had no proper kit or shoes.

However, for the first few days the country was flattish and it was fairly easy going. The children couldn't understand what was happening, and when we started they thought it was quite fun. Not so Treve—he was used to jungle travel and didn't at all like the restriction of the canvas hammock in which, as he was still only four years old, he was supposed to travel. Neither did he like the strange faces of the coolies who were carrying him. In fact, at this juncture, he was one of the most complaining of the children; to the others it was all rather new and exciting.

For me, except for the extraordinary circumstances, it was much like normal jungle touring. Every family had its own tent, and where possible we camped near Forest Rest Houses which gave us extra accommodation. The worry was that every day was getting hotter. At this time of year, as a rule, we should never have attempted a jungle march.

We were making first for Tamu, a small town near the borders of Manipur and about six day's march through the jungle from Mawlaik. Jim decided not to take the main well-worn track, for there were streams of Indian evacuees swarming along it in an attempt to get back to their own country. Not only would the dust have been choking, but our elephants would have congested things and hampered progress; so we struck off on side paths, which were pleasanter too for us because it was thicker jungle and more shaded from the sun.

Each morning when we left, Jim stayed behind to see the elephants being loaded. Then, once he had got them off on their way, he pushed ahead on foot to look for a suitable camping site for the next night. As he passed by he would give me a word of encouragement, but he was so busy that that was about all I saw of him, except when we settled down at night.

He was having quite a difficult time with his elephants, who were used to wandering off and foraging for themselves when the day's work was done. Now, on this forced march, they had to be ready at hand, and at nights they were tied up and fed by the oozies. This restriction made them restive and irritable and they kept trying to break loose, which was a big worry to Jim, for if any of them had stampeded it would have caused havoc in our camp.

The general spirit amongst everyone at this time was pretty good; in fact, now we had started, and the waiting was over, everyone seemed determined to put a cheerful face on it. We were very conscious of the children among us too, and concentrated on trying to keep them happy.

The only slightly bad feeling, perhaps, was about the pitching of the tents; everyone naturally wanted theirs to be out of the heat of the sun for the sake of their children. By the time we all arrived on the scene each day, Jim had chosen the sites and got the tents up. Ours was invariably in the hottest spot, and I mentioned this to Jim one night.

He said that naturally he always had to pick the worst place for us—being in charge, he could hardly do otherwise—and I at once saw his point. The very fact that I had even brought it up was, I think, a sign of the weariness that was already making itself felt.

Six days later we reached Tamu. Jim as usual had gone ahead of us and was supervising the unloading, and getting the tents erected near the outskirts of the little town. Quite suddenly, and for no apparent reason, one of the huge tusker elephants attacked the head Burman in charge of the oozies, and knelt on him. He was killed outright.

Jim was deeply disturbed by this tragedy and tried to keep it from the main party when we walked in, hot and tired, about an hour later; but inevitably the news leaked out, and a great gloom was cast over everybody.

Jim noticed particularly that the morale of the Burmans was very shaken and he made the decision there and then that male elephants were too uncertain companions to have with us on this march, and that they must be dropped; for the rest of the way we should continue only with females, who were much less temperamental. This, of course, meant that the carrying capacity was greatly reduced.

He called us all together and explained the situation, telling us that from now on only one small suitcase would be allowed for each person. Some of the wives, who had been living on the spot in Mawlaik when we had started, had naturally tried to bring all they could from their homes there. I remember seeing one of them carrying out a canteen of silver and installing it in the hammock with her baby. Another had a beautiful green morocco leather fitted dressing case, which she clung to like grim death as it had been her husband's wedding present to her.

Nearly everyone, in fact, had managed to load some of the things they treasured most onto the elephants, and it came as a shock that these precious possessions now had to be abandoned. After this we felt more like the bunch of evacuees which, in fact, we were.

Jim broke it to us too that from here onwards we should be walking on narrow mule tracks through mountainous country;

he told us it would be hard for us all. The simpler comforts we had had so far, such as tents, camp beds, etc., would not be practicable now, as there would be no place to pitch them, and the elephants would be unable to carry anything but absolute necessities.

We all made the most of that last day under canvas. Clothes were washed, and the children were given a good bath, as no one knew from now on what the water situation was going to be like.

Jim sent two men ahead to find this out, and also to see what food grew on the way for the elephants. The reports that came back were far from favourable, and he thought at one moment that the elephants might have to be discarded altogether; however, it was decided that we must take the risk, and shoot the animals later if necessary.

As the women piled up the belongings they had to abandon, they still chatted optimistically to each other about how they would collect them again when things got better. Unlike most of the others, we had no possessions with us to leave behind in Tamu, but at this juncture there was a very sad parting for us.

Dear old Joseph, and Jim's faithful Aung Net, had come with us so far, and there was no thought in either of their heads other than to stay with us, but the situation had begun to make us both anxious. If we all got through safely we should, we hoped, be able to live in India for the time being, but these men had families left behind in Maymyo. If the worst happened, and Burma was overrun by the Japs, how would they ever get back to them?

"The moment has come," said Jim, "to tell them they must return. The farther we take them on, the more difficult their journey back will become."

They had both been with Jim since he first came out to Burma twenty years before, and it was a hard moment for all three of them. When they came to say goodbye to me, we were none of us able to say a word. I think we all felt that this was the beginning of the break up.

Jim felt that nothing he could do could reward these two men for all they had done for him. He gave them all he could raise at this moment, which amounted to about a year's pay each. Aung Net was such a guileless character that Jim warned him to tell no one he was carrying this money as they travelled home.

They went marching off together through the trees, without a backward look, and that was the last we ever heard or saw of them.

There was also San Pyu, who had worked for us in Mawlaik and was here with us. Jim had wanted him to return with the others, but he was an orphan, and as he had no ties he begged to be allowed to come on. Treve was devoted to him and was also anxious for him to stay with us, so we agreed.

CHAPTER XXVI

REFUGEE CAVALCADE

WITH comforts gone, each day our tempers became less sweet. The track began to ascend precipitously into the mountains of Manipur—rocky and narrow, in places it was hardly wide enough for a loaded elephant to get along. We had to go in single file all the way. All the time news was coming over the wireless that the Japs were advancing further into Burma, and we were urged to hurry, but this was not easy for our cumbersome procession of grown-ups, children and elephants up and down these heights.

We were not by ourselves any longer now, as strings of Indian refugees were trying to pass us all the time. Some carried tin boxes on their heads containing all their possessions, while others had small children perched on their shoulders or dragging along by their sides. All trudged onwards towards the same goal—India.

Treve could not understand the rush. Much earlier on, before we had started climbing, we had had to give way and allow him to get out of his hammock and walk, and then he was immediately much happier. But as the way got steeper, I couldn't imagine he would be able to keep it up much longer. However, I was wrong, for he did in fact walk nearly the whole of the hundred and seventy miles.

Fate, in its haphazard way, sometimes does one a good turn. As time went on we came more and more to realise that without San Pyu, the orphan lad, the way would have been much harder, especially for Treve.

San Pyu did not look at first glance the sort of person whom one would have chosen for support in a situation such as this. He was slight in build, and the hand was missing from his right arm—he had been born with only a stump, about which he was self-conscious, hardly ever allowing it to be seen. But his courage was not easily to be forgotten, and he was always unobtrusively there just when needed.

If we had to climb a particularly sheer escarpment he was ready just ahead to heave me up with his stick, and before Treve had time to be apprehensive he had whisked him into the air and onto his shoulder, and had him laughing at the joke. Although Treve hated being carried, he sometimes allowed San Pyu, for whom he too had a glowing admiration, to take him on his shoulders and jog along with him for a mile or so.

We had to move on each morning at about four o'clock so that the elephants could get away early while the bridle track was comparatively clear. Having suffered from heat for the first six days down on the plains, up here in the mountains the cold was our trouble.

At this hour of the morning everything was wreathed in damp mist, with an icy wind blowing down from the snow-capped peaks beyond. Getting the children up was the worst part, and we could hear their cries all round as they were hauled out of their warm blankets; they hated being woken up in the dark in this bleak and windy place.

Everyone felt the cold, and there was no conversation at all as we had something to eat and got ready to move on as quickly as possible. We were fortunate in having some shelter along the way—the tea companies having hurriedly started putting up a few huts here and there for refugees. But the building had only just begun and most of the huts had no roofs, and they were all open to the weather; however, they served as wind breaks and we were grateful for them. Unfortunately, by the time we arrived some of them had been used by hordes of refugees before us, and the filth and excrement we found had to be dealt with before we could settle down.

Naw Lah rose above it all. Her imperturbable personality seemed equal to any strain, and I never heard her complain. With her sleek black hair swept back into a shiny bun, and her beautiful skin, she always gave the impression of being well groomed, and it did one good to look at her.

As we trekked on, some of the women who were expecting babies began to get terribly exhausted—especially those in late pregnancy. One in particular, whose child was due very soon, had to give in and be carried on an improvised stretcher. I felt very thankful that my baby was not expected for another six months; no one except Jim even knew it was on the way, and I was able to carry on normally.

One is able to learn from every situation that life presents. This march opened my eyes and made me understand a little how great strain and exhaustion can play havoc for the time being with the ordinary decent personality.

During the first days of the journey—and even then conditions were quite difficult—one was cheered by the thoughtfulness and consideration people showed to each other; but as things got harder, the mothers, while remaining unselfish for themselves, began to get grasping on their children's behalf.

I remember one day catching sight of an old mountain peasant with a few bananas and one or two eggs, and my immediate thought was, 'How can I get them all for Treve?' As it happened, we were all so crushed together that this wasn't possible, but that was the sort of thought which now began to be uppermost in one's mind. Similarly, when Evelyn Bostock and I were doling out the food, we noticed that a few people would try to come round twice, before everyone else had had their turn.

Instinctively, people were reserving all the strength they had left to keep their children and themselves going, and they began to feel that the little extra to give away to others was simply not there. We came, for instance, to a place on the mountainside which was so sheer that, on looking down, I was overcome with giddiness and could not attempt it for the moment and so I sat on a rock and let them all pass me. If this had happened earlier on, the others would have turned as they went by to ask if all was well, but I noticed that no one turned their head—they simply hadn't noticed, and wouldn't have cared if they had.

It is at times like this that the really exceptional spirit shines forth and, as always, there were those amongst us who set such an inspiring example that it infused itself through the whole party and kept us going.

There was one girl in her early twenties, with two children, who at the beginning had been so quiet and mouselike that we had had the feeling she was not going to be a great deal of help when times got worse. How mistaken we were—her serenity never altered, and one gradually found oneself seeking her company in order to borrow some of her strength. She was alone with her two children, but they were the happiest of the lot, and soon other people's children began to gather round her, too.

One evening we settled down to camp after one of the worst day's marching. The children were dispirited and so tired that they were almost beyond consoling—they couldn't understand why they were being put through all this. Then the young woman got her scissors and started cutting out dolls' clothes from various odd scraps she had gathered together. Soon she had sitting round her a circle of grimy, weary little beings, completely forgetting their troubles for one glorious half hour before being rolled up in their blankets and put to sleep.

We had now climbed to 5,000 feet, and Jim was having difficulty in finding suitable places for us to camp. Water was the problem; to find enough for us and for his elephants was quite a job, for elephants are heavy drinkers, but the time came when they had to be tied up for the night without any.

I remember Jim taking a bucket to a trickle which he found on the mountainside. The flow was so feeble that it took over half an hour to fill it, and the small amount of water he got had to be rationed between forty of us.

Washing, of course, was out of the question. This didn't worry the children much—Treve never liked washing at the best of times—but it had not helped our morale to see one another getting more jaded and untidy each day, and the thought that we were now also going to be dirty and unwashed was really depressing.

Jim, as always, gave everyone new heart. Once again, it was his gift for having faith in others and at the same time faith in himself that made everybody feel they must give of their best, and induced a sure confidence amongst us that he would get us all safely through in the end.

It was not to any of the women that the mothers would go when they needed advice or consolation, but to him.

"My little boy has had an upset stomach for three days and won't eat—what shall I do?"

"I find I can't stop shivering at night—what do you think is the matter?"

"What do you think will happen to my husband now the Japs are closing in on Rangoon?"

These were the sort of questions he considered patiently and answered to the best of his ability. I never saw him appear to be hurried or irritable with them, and the only thing that used to get him down a little, and then he never showed it, was when some of the more thoughtless women insisted on telling him almost every day how lucky he was to be here with us when their husbands had had to stay behind.

The plight of the elephants, though, was really beginning to worry him; they badly needed water, and had been twenty-four hours without it. The problem was partially solved when the oozies, in their constant search for it, came upon a group of peasants' houses with a small banana plantation nearby. When Jim heard of this, he ordered them to go at once and cut the whole lot down, compensating the villagers for their loss. He hoped that the juicy banana stems would quench the elephants' thirst slightly, as well as giving them nourishment.

With the water supply precarious, the swarms of flies which

buzzed around us all the time brought an ever present risk of cholera. As the stream of refugees increased, this became a real danger, and we knew a lot of them were dying from it on the way. Although we had all been injected against cholera while waiting at Mawlaik, every precaution was now taken, and whenever food was doled out huge mosquito nets were hung over everybody while they ate.

Jim had been hard at it with very little chance for sleep for about ten days, when one night, just after we had settled down, a messenger who had been with a group of travellers ahead came back. He told Jim that cholera was spreading among the Indians, and that six of them had died on the path ahead of us. Their companions had hurried on, leaving them where they were.

It was already dark, but Jim took his torch and set out along the two miles of craggy track to where this had happened. He was determined that these bodies must be got out of the way before we passed by next morning. The messenger helped him to find the spot where they lay, but there was no chance of burial, and together they had to roll them into the deep ravine below. Not a word was said, and when we went by that way the next day, no one was any the wiser.

Chapter XXVII

RELENTLESS MARCH

IT was not the distance of this journey but the relentlessness of the country that wore us down. Every day we seemed to have to descend one side of a mountain in order immediately to start climbing the next one in front of us. Sometimes the way seemed absolutely perpendicular, so that, if we had had that amount of humour left, we should have thought of ourselves as flies climbing up a wall.

As we struggled up, we longed for the moment of reaching the top and being able to descend again, but the jarring movement and the concentration needed to pick one's way down these rocky gorges soon made one think that the going up had been easier.

Above all we longed to stop, and felt that if only we could be allowed a day or two's rest all would be well. Now we were no longer worried by thoughts of possessions left behind, or of what our life was to be ahead. There were only two words to which we had to cling tenaciously—*keep going*.

Despite the fact that we were trudging along in a sort of daze, I quite well remember appreciating how magnificent this country was—dramatic and ruthless in its wildness and grandeur. We were walking along narrow paths carved out of the rock face; nothing much grew here as we were above tree level, but we could look down onto the tops of the fir trees hundreds of feet below. They formed a deep greeny blue carpet below us which stretched away into the far distance.

I said to Jim one night, "Before we die we must come back here for a holiday."

A pile of logs that only elephants
could disentangle

Jim with Susan,
a fortnight before
his death

Treve on a jungle trek, with
San Pyu in foreground

He laughed and said, "Good God, I shouldn't have thought you would want to set eyes on it ever again!"

Occasionally I would see flowers growing in inaccessible places, and as Jim was going ahead of us one day, I handed him a little bunch of white violets. I had been astonished to find them growing up here, and when I saw them hiding so modestly under their leaves by the side of the track it had brought England back to me with such a sharp pang that I had been unable to pass them by.

Jim told me afterwards that as he had walked on up through the pathetic procession of plodding children, the scent of these little flowers gave him a tremendous lift and encouragement. In later years he often reminded me of this episode.

He was hurrying ahead now, because he had heard that further along the route the British Army were working with bulldozers on preliminary measures for widening the way. There were endless rumours of what the army's plans were, but the thought uppermost in Jim's mind was how our elephants were going to pass the machines on this precipitous track, only a few feet wide. The sight of the bulldozer alone, apart from its noise, would be enough to make them stampede.

He located a British subaltern, whose machine was perched at a most dangerous angle as he forced his way along the face of the escarpment, and it was arranged that he should halt work while we passed. Luckily, a wide enough place was found for the elephants to walk round the bulldozer, which they did later without turning a hair.

Twelve days after, we thankfully made our last mountainside descent and the plains lay stretched out in front of us for hundreds of miles ahead. For all the dust and heat, the knowledge that we should now be walking on the flat came as a consolation after all the climbing up and down we had done. However, after even one day's walking on these plains, some people were already saying how much better it had been going over the mountains.

Refugees were tramping in a long stream away into the distance as far as the eye could see, and raising clouds of red dust with every step they took. This particularly worried the children, as it got in their eyes and throats and made them cough. The stuff penetrated everywhere, and after a while we all looked like Red Indians.

Jim held up a little looking-glass for Treve. "Look at yourself: you really are an Indian chief now," he said.

I tied something on his head to try to complete the picture and to amuse him, but he just hung his head—utterly weary, and too done in to be diverted.

Treve's determination all the way so far had made me very proud, and brought home to me that character does not only develop with age, but is largely innate. Many of the children here displayed tremendous fortitude and set an example to people very much older.

He had lost a good deal of weight, but seemed to be well on the whole. All the same, I felt more than relieved that Tom's children were safely with him in India, and had escaped all this. We were still hoping that later on we should somehow be able to pick them up again.

Lying in the middle of the plains was a small place called Palel, and by the time we arrived there we must have looked a miserable bunch. I had lost well over a stone in weight, and so must most of the others as I noticed that their clothes were hanging loosely round them.

By great luck we found that the British Army had a unit working here—and how glad we were to see them. The more so as they took pity on us, and arranged with Jim that they would assign two or three army lorries to transport us over the next hundred and sixty miles to Dimapur, and the railway.

We were a very thankful lot of people as we piled in, one on top of the other, with our dusty bedding rolls and belongings, which had been unloaded from the elephants, heaped amongst us.

The elephants, too, must have heaved a sigh of relief when

we reached Palel. During the last part of the march their condition had deteriorated badly, but they had all survived. Here there was plenty of green food for them to eat growing round about, and at long last they were allowed to wander off to find it for themselves. There was a river, too, with enough water for them to bathe in and drink to their hearts' content. We had to leave their oozies behind, but Jim told them he would be back in about four days, when he and Geoff Bostock had seen us on to the train at Dimapur.

We spent that night in Imphal, in a large refugee camp which had been set up by one of the tea companies to house the hundreds of evacuees as they journeyed through. It consisted of huge bamboo matting sheds, rather like aeroplane hangars, and inside a bamboo platform about eight feet square was allotted to each family.

Naw Lah, Jim, Treve and I piled up onto ours. It was not much of a place but, in spite of the crowds around us and the heat, at least it was our own for the time being. The highlight of the evening was that almost everybody was able to get a hot bath in a tin tub—no marble bathroom had ever seemed so inviting.

A Mr. and Mrs. Shaw were running this shelter, and a wonderful job they made of it. We felt thankful to them from the bottom of our hearts for feeding us and giving us refuge, and we were greatly distressed later when we heard that the place had been completely blotted out by Japanese bombs, and that Mrs. Shaw had been killed as well as a great many refugees.

Here there was to be yet another sad parting. We did not know until we reached Imphal that a war-time regulation had been made forbidding Burmans to cross the border into India. The authorities gave permission for Naw Lah to continue with us, but refused a permit for our faithful companion, the boy San Pyu. We were extremely anxious about this orphan lad's prospects, and Jim did everything he could to persuade the officials to change their minds.

San Pyu felt himself to be very much part of our household, and above all he could not bear the thought of saying goodbye to Treve. But Jim's efforts were of no avail; the best he could arrange was for San Pyu to wait here until he picked him up again on his return to Burma. He looked forlorn and lost, standing there next morning, as with heavy hearts we waved goodbye.

From Imphal our lorries took us the hundred and thirty miles to Dimapur, and as we saw the road climbing up into the mountains again we felt we should never have had the strength to continue this part of the journey on foot. The fact that there was a road at all was because in 1893 the Maharajah of Manipur had been forced to construct it as a reprisal for the massacre of several British officers during a rebellion. Before that it had only been a bridle track.

It was a fantastic drive and in places frightening, as the road was cut from the sheer face of the cliff, with drops of thousands of feet to the valleys below. Later in the war there were many casualties among army lorries that had misjudged the bends and gone hurtling over the side.

Eighty-seven miles along the road we passed through the small township of Kohima. At this moment it was bathed in peaceful sunshine, and the houses set on the hillside were smothered in pink rambler roses. The residents waved to us as we passed—their turn for upheaval had not yet come.

It was not until just over two years later that the Japs arrived at this point and cut all roads into the town, isolating it. The British and Indian garrison clung to this battered place for fifty days and nights until they were relieved. Their magnificent stand at Kohima stopped the Japanese march on Delhi and was one of the starting points of the victorious advance back into Burma.

To sit in the railway carriage at Dimapur railway station with the march over was the moment we had all longed for, but now, when we were actually in the train, we were too tired to appreciate it. We just sank into heavy heaps and most people dropped off to sleep immediately, with the consoling thought at the back of their minds that they did not have to move again for the next two days.

On looking back, what happened next seems almost comic—at the time it came as absolutely the last straw. The train was shunting backwards, before moving out of the station—it went a bit too fast, and was derailed. Bags and bundles fell on our heads, and the children were thrown on to the ground.

At this moment we simply could not take it, and stoical as all these people had been on the way, when much worse was happening, many of them just broke down and wept.

Poor Jim—he had thought he had got us all safely off his hands, and here we were derailed only a hundred yards down the track, and unable to go off that night. Coming down the siding, he climbed into the carriage and with a look of utter dejection said, "This is the ruddy end."

He sank down in the carriage with us for about ten minutes, and then he was off again, organising arrangements for us all to be fed in the meantime.

Next morning I had to say goodbye to him, and as he stood on the platform ready to wave us off I felt deeply worried. I could see he was worn out, and the thought that he now had to do the same long journey all the way back was more than I could bear.

But he was determined to go. He had twenty elephants and their oozies waiting for him at Palel, and he knew that they were all-important. It had been considered impossible for them to carry out this difficult trek with its deprivations; now that they had achieved it once, Jim felt that it was literally a matter of life and death for the refugees left behind that these elephants should be used to carry food and medical supplies out to them.

The train was about to move off. "Don't worry," said Jim. "I feel the main burden is off my shoulders now that you are all safely here—we'll meet up again sometime soon."

His brother Nick was living in Calcutta, and he was happy to think that Treve and I were going to him and would be taken care of.

*   *   *

In describing this march out of Burma, I realise acutely how fortunate our lot was compared with that of so many of those who came after. At the time it seemed hard, especially as then we did not know what the outcome would be; but compared with the thousands of people who left their homes in unorganised parties, many of them quite alone, we were indeed lucky. It was not until much later that we heard of the terrible sufferings experienced by those who had to start their journeys at the beginning of the rains—it was next to hopeless, and hundreds of them perished in the attempt.

It was the Bombay Burmah Corporation that we had to thank for planning and organising our march in the early days of the Japanese advance into Burma. At the time they were criticized for being panicky, but by their foresight they certainly saved the lives of a great many of their employees and their families, and also of many other helpless refugee travellers.

Chapter XXVIII

ELEPHANT LEADER

TREVE, Naw Lah and I were most kindly received and wonderfully looked after in Calcutta, but after a week in Nick's comfortable flat we moved on again. A friend of his had a house in the Khasi Hills, near Shillong in Assam, and wrote offering to share it with us. I gratefully accepted.

We faced up to the necessity of a long train journey through India to Assansol in order to fetch Tom's children, and then we all travelled there together. It was delightful to arrive, and to feel that we could settle down, for a time at least. The climate was lovely, and there were schools for the children.

I was glad to have found so peaceful a place for them, but I could not really enjoy it myself—the general situation was too sad. Rangoon had now fallen and the British Army under General Alexander was in full retreat. I felt it was all wrong that I should be so comfortable while Burma, and the people in it we had loved, were in such turmoil.

Another anxiety was that Jim was still on the march with the refugees. Messages came through from time to time for the next two months, giving me news of him. On his way back, he and the untiring Geoff Bostock had built an evacuee camp which they ran together for six weeks. He then had gone backwards and forwards many times over the track on which we had marched, arranging for supplies. The elephants which had brought us out were safely returned all the way back to Tamu, just over the Burma border; Jim told me that this little town, where we had stayed before starting on our long climb, was now stark with tragedy. Refugees were pouring in from all quarters and at one time there were two thousand four hundred Indians in the place, and only eight bags of rice to feed them on.

Eventually the rains came, and halted the human tide completely. Tragedy and death were everywhere, but there was little that could be done to help.

Once Rangoon had fallen, in March 1942, it meant the collapse of Burma, and in this new situation the teak company seconded Jim to the Assam Government, to survey the timber there and in Bengal. It was the greatest joy when the job brought him back to me, in Shillong. When Treve and I had arrived there, we had had hardly anything to wear; Jim literally had nothing but what he stood up in. He was very thin, but otherwise fit.

Soon after he arrived my baby was born—a little girl. We decided to call her Lamorna, after the beautiful cove near Jim's home in Cornwall. Her arrival gave Naw Lah a new lease of life—she was thrilled to have another infant to look after. Treve was nearly five now, and very grown up for his years, but he adored Naw Lah—as he and Lamorna still do to this day.

Jim went on one trip into the Assam jungle, to reconnoitre for timber, but most of his time was spent in an office near where we were living in Shillong. He became very restless, and longed to be more closely connected with the drive to save Burma, feeling strongly that elephants would have to play a much larger part if a real effort to regain the country were to be made.

The Army evidently realised this too, for General Irwin, G.O.C. Eastern Army, sent for him to go to Calcutta. He went off at once and three days later a wire came from him: "Have been offered army job—leave it to you whether I accept."

Needless to say, I wired back at once: "Go ahead."

A few weeks later he was installed with the Intelligence branch at headquarters in Imphal, Manipur. He had more detailed knowledge of the Burma jungle, especially in the

Chindwin area, than most people, and with his photographic memory his advice at Army Headquarters was invaluable. They appreciated that elephants were of the first importance and appointed him there and then Elephant Adviser (with the rank of Lieutenant-Colonel) to the Fourteenth Army—the only trouble being that when the Japs had finally overrun Burma they had captured all Jim's elephants, even the ones that had been used to carry our kit on the march out. So for the moment the title was a bit of a misnomer, and he got very teased about it.

Eventually he persuaded the commanding officer to give him a jeep and let him go to Tamu, to see if he could salvage any elephants which had not fallen into Japanese hands. When the British had pulled out, the Burmese oozies had refused to abandon their elephants and took them home with them to their native villages. Only under threats and bribes did the Japanese manage to muster a corps of about two thousand.

As he neared Burma, Jim heard that a group of forty captured elephants were being moved by the Japanese through the jungle to Mawlaik, and he managed to send a message through to the oozies saying that, if they would divert them to Tamu, which had not yet fallen, he would be there to meet them. This they did, with great courage, travelling by night through Japanese-infested jungle.

When they arrived, Jim was surprised to see that some of the elephants were being ridden by women. The oozies explained that when his message came through, many of the elephants were without riders; they had been about to abandon them, but they and their families were so heartened to hear from him that they had persuaded their wives to ride the spare animals and come too.

It was a thrilling moment for everybody. Jim now had forty elephants to advise on, and this group was the first of what later became known as No. I Elephant Company, Royal Indian Engineers.

In his books Jim has related the exploits of his elephants

with the Fourteenth Army much better than I am able to do. By underground methods he soon managed to collect about one hundred and twenty of them together, and they were in constant demand for clearing the way, building bridges and making roads. All sorts of different army services wanted their help, and some ridiculous and impossible requests were made.

Jim used to tell the story of how someone came to ask him for an elephant to spray tar along the road with its trunk. I doubt very much whether that was true, but I do know for a fact that he was asked for an elephant to crank up a jeep.

At the beginning of 1943, Jim was sent for to meet Orde Wingate, who was then a Brigadier; he wanted advice about what the conditions were likely to be on the raiding operations he was about to undertake into the heart of Burma. Jim was able to help him about the lay-out of the jungle, and with such important details as where he would find water for his troops and his animals.

Wingate and his men later crossed the Chindwin and completed the first phase of their mission with speed and precision; but difficulties began to accumulate. He had to abandon his plan for destroying the Mandalay-Lashio Railway, and by June 1943 the expedition was over.

It had been one of the most heroic enterprises of all time. The officers and men of Wingate's army had marched about a thousand miles in roughly ten weeks. Their way lay through the thick of the jungle without any paths to follow—each man carrying on his back a pack weighing about half his own weight—in the intense humid heat to start with, and ending up in the horror of the rains.

Before the war few of these men had been regular soldiers; nearly all were ordinary civilians called up into the army. From the beginning Jim had thought that their task was a hopeless one—a third of them did not return, and many who did never fully recovered their health.

But their achievements were many. Having smashed up a vital line of communications in Burma and arrested the

Japanese threat to the north, they had confused the enemy's plans and diverted a large number of his troops, many times their own strength. Above all, they had gained invaluable experience necessary for the next stage of the war.

The fortunes of battle swung to and fro and, for the second time, late in 1943 the Fourteenth Army was pushed back yet again—this time right back to Imphal in the plains of Manipur. Jim lost a great many of his elephants in this retreat, but he managed to reach Imphal with about forty-five of them, together with their oozies and their families.

Imphal was then in a state of siege. Full of soldiers and refugees, the small town was bulging at the seams. Jim's forty-five elephants were anything but an asset under the circumstances, and feeding them was next to impossible. He was informed that they must be got out somehow and kept safely until they were needed again.

Jim made a plan which, at the time, he thought was almost an impossible one, but there was no alternative. He decided to try and take them to Assam, over a hundred miles away, with the help of three of his officers. All the roads out of Imphal were cut, but there was a foot track to the west, and from the map he could see that if he went this way it would mean crossing five ranges of mountains, of six thousand feet and over, through almost impenetrable jungle.

Having made up his mind to embark on this extremely hazardous attempt to get his elephants to safety, at the last minute he was told he must take with him a party of sixty-four Gurkha women and children who were stranded in Imphal. This was more than he had bargained for, but it had to be done.

No one had much hope of the party getting through. They were given a red parachute to spread out each night, so that their route could be followed from the air—in fact, they were never spotted.

The women and children were a seedy lot even when they started. Many of the sick had to be carried, and how the rest of them managed to do it Jim never knew. In many places it was more a matter of climbing than of walking.

At the very beginning, after struggling for two miles up hill through dense undergrowth and bamboo, they suddenly came upon the perpendicular face of a cliff, about three hundred feet high, standing sheer in front of them. No way round it could be found, and this seemed the end; the party had to halt for two days whilst it was decided what to do next.

There was nothing for it but to try to cut steps into the sandstone cliff face. Earlier on Jim had noticed a narrow ledge about two hundred and fifty feet up—a slip in the escarpment—and he felt that if his elephants could reach this they might be able to climb the rest of the way in safety.

All available hands worked the whole of the following two days to hack a way up. By now Jim had come to have a belief in tackling the impossible. He told me afterwards that at the time he could not imagine any of the people being able to balance themselves up this ghastly stone ladder—as for the elephants doing it, he had practically no hope at all.

What a merciful thing it was that among the elephants was the wonderful Bandoola with his oozie, Po Toke. Jim had crawled down after a last inspection of the steps, and had come to the conclusion that no elephant would ever be induced to attempt them.

Po Toke, who was standing near, must have sensed his feeling of despair. "All will be well tomorrow, Thakin," he said; and added with quiet confidence, "Bandoola will lead."

Next morning brought one of the most memorable moments in Jim's life with elephants. At dawn he went ahead by himself, climbing the two hundred and fifty feet up to the ledge on all fours all the way. The women and children squatted on the sand at the base of the cliff, waiting. There was utter silence.

Po Toke rode Bandoola, with his great white tusks, up to the high wall of stone and faced him to it. Then in a low voice he said firmly:

"Climb."

Bandoola lifted his two forefeet onto the first step: it was just wide enough to take them. Then with infinite precision and balance, but also with much difficulty, he drew up his hindquarters, squeezing the toenails of his back feet in behind, on the same step.

As if it had been a carefully rehearsed circus act he balanced where he was for nearly nine minutes before he was sure enough to make the next move. Everyone thought he was about to topple backwards. Then with a tremendous effort he drew his front feet up again to the next step.

To the breathless astonishment of all watching, he eventually did the whole lot, taking two and a half hours to reach the top. So great was the strain that his leg muscles quivered for about an hour afterwards.

Po Toke had known that if one elephant could be found with the courage and cleverness to show the way, the rest would follow. He also knew that Bandoola, his hero, must lead. One by one all forty-five animals climbed the perilous stairway and reached the high ridge above. Somehow, in a sort of precarious shuttle service, the oozies then pulled and carried the women and children up the precipice too.

It was a tremendous achievement for Jim and his officers when the way-worn band of people finally marched into Assam. The last part of the journey had been even worse than the first, and everyone was so exhausted that it was only by constant encouragement that they could manage the final stretch. The expedition had taken six days longer than Jim had expected, and for the last week rations were down to half a cigarette-tin of rice per day for each person.

There was much illness too, and malaria was rife. None of them, including the elephants, had ever been up to such heights before, and man and beast suffered badly from cold and exposure. The Army had given up the expedition for lost, as never once in that mountainous jungle country had they been able to spot the red parachute when it had been laid out each evening.

Of all the elephants Bandoola suffered least, and Jim described to me what a thoroughbred he looked as he strode out of the dense jungle into the sunlight of an Assam tea garden. On his back was a load of very sick young Gurkha children— their heads hanging over the edge of the carrier. As Jim saw their pale faces he had a lump in his throat, and said a prayer of thankfulness that they would soon be safe in hospital and able to get the medical attention they so badly needed.

Chapter XXIX

ELEPHANTS AT WAR

I HAD heard a rumour that Jim was on his way to Assam but couldn't conceive by what means he was to get here. I little thought that he would be coming with his elephants over mountains higher than even Hannibal had attempted, and through jungle which had rarely been penetrated before.

When he arrived at our house he looked as thin as a scarecrow. Apart from anything else, he had been suffering for the last year from symptoms of an acute duodenal ulcer, and almost immediately he had to go into hospital for treatment. He was very frustrated at being laid up for six weeks during this important phase of the war.

While in hospital a fellow patient, a *Times* War Correspondent, was so entertained by his elephant stories that he suggested to Jim that he should try to write some of them down. This he did, and although at the time he had no thought of publishing them, they were in fact the substance of what later became his book *Elephant Bill*.

From the early days of the War in Burma, when Jim had first formed his Elephant Company, he had been nicknamed Elephant Bill by his companions, and now he was known by this name throughout the Fourteenth Army. The Japs too knew him well by repute and Jim found out later that he was well up on their list of wanted persons to be captured dead or alive.

As soon as he came out of hospital he reported for duty at Army Headquarters and then went to pick up his elephants which for the past six weeks had been resting on the plains below. They had been in such poor condition after the long march from Imphal that unless they had been given this time in which to recuperate they would have been no further use in the war.

Meanwhile the Japanese offensive continued. The elephants that they had captured were now an essential part of their war machine and were perfect for carrying their main weapon in the rapid advance—the mortar and its ammunition. They could climb mountains inaccessible to wheel transport, could move forward in daylight through forests, undetected by aircraft, and were capable of long night marches.

It was now April 1944, and the battle for Imphal raged. It was here that the Japanese expected to make their final onslaught. They brought forward all their forces and at least a thousand elephants were used, many of them being shot by air attack, a task which the pilots of the R.A.F. and the U.S.A.A.F. thoroughly disliked.

The fortress was assaulted by the Japs with everything they had, but a wall of resistance rose in their path; the Air Force had flown in huge reinforcements of men and supplies to the besieged army, and in the end the place was to become not so much a defended base as an offensive springboard. The tide then turned, the enemy were in full retreat, and by December the jungle war had been won by the British and Indian troops of the Fourteenth Army, and 50,000 Japanese lay dead.

"In this year," said General Slim, "we have smashed the Japanese soldier—now in the next year we shall smash the Japanese Army."

When the siege was over, Jim's elephants were needed more than ever for the big push back. To his joy, he found that a young Anglo-Indian, who had been cut off during the Japanese offensive, had been able to find and reassemble some of those animals which had been abandoned months before. Their oozies had successfully hidden them from the enemy, and soon they were hard at work again; not for transport now, as the monsoon was just ending and the Fourteenth Army were advancing on wheels; but they had terrible mud to cope with and the elephants were invaluable for releasing vehicles bogged down in swamps. Jim said he had sometimes watched them pulling lorries out of the mud as though they were drawing corks out of champagne bottles.

Their main service, as always, was bridge building and they went about their work with the precision of a carpenter. They also helped with the evacuation of the wounded, carrying sick men many miles over roads which were impassable even for mules.

Elephants had proved themselves throughout to be as adaptable in the tumult of war as they were in peace. It was astonishing what they could achieve, working quite undisturbed alongside bulldozers and other machines. All this was not through fear, but through loyal obedience to their oozies. Elephants in any case are not nervous beasts, but they can be startled just like any other animal; they may sometimes appear to be nervous, but that is perhaps because there is much more of an elephant to be startled.

At first when aircraft flew low over them they would trumpet loudly, but they soon became quite used to this, calmly collecting supplies dropped from the air. They came to know that among these supplies was their ration of salt; in peacetime they could find this for themselves in the jungle, but now they were tethered and it had to be provided for them.

Jim felt sure that if elephants were used in any jungle war of the future, they would probably be glided in, just as Wingate's mules were, by the glider forces. But whether the veterinary surgeons would ever be able to stop the elephants' trumpeting as Wingate's mules were stopped braying by silencing their vocal cords, is another matter.

Jim was inordinately proud of his elephants' achievements. Like them, he had had to adapt himself to the wartime jungle, and he did not always find it easy to conform to army routine. Sometimes the authorities were annoyed by his independent spirit. For instance he had always been used to wearing shorts and he continued to do so now, although it was against regulations.

"If it's malaria they are frightened about," he said, "I am hardened to that by now. I like my tot of rum, too, and I am sure the mosquitoes would fall off drunk if they tried to feed off me!"

Altogether he and the other officers and men of his elephant companies managed to recapture 1,652 elephants from the enemy and now that the tables had turned they were in constant use against them. While in Japanese hands these animals had suffered many tragedies of their own—they had been bombed from the air and blown up by land mines. Regardless of their physical needs, they had been pushed to the utmost limits and made to carry almost impossible loads. The Japanese had a passion for ivory, and had sawn off most of the elephants' tusks as souvenirs, thus greatly reducing their capacity for manœuvring timber.

The saddest casualty of all, as far as Jim was concerned, was Bandoola. He was found one day lying in a clearing in the forest with a bullet through his brain. Po Toke came to Jim in camp, tears streaming down his face, to tell him the news. They went together to the spot where he lay. It was a tragic sight to see this fine animal lying in the mud, even now starting to decompose, and with his right tusk missing.

His remaining tusk was carefully removed and was one of Jim's most prized possessions for the rest of his life. We kept it in our home, where we were able to see it and remember its gallant owner and his heroism for always.

*　　　*　　　*

By May 1945 Rangoon had been recaptured and the war in Burma was virtually over, except for mopping-up operations. When unconditional surrender finally came, the elephants were disbanded and gradually returned to their peacetime work in the forests again. But these working herds had suffered heavy casualties and were very much diminished and the political situation was now too unsettled for them to be replenished by captures from wild herds. Indeed it was doubtful if existing wild herds were even capable of supplying the needs. The animal-man relationship too, which had been so unique in the largest timber companies, would have to have been built up all over again.

For a short time after the war the firms tried to struggle on operating the timber forests in Burma, but soon organisation became impossible. Stolen arms had fallen into the wrong hands, and the jungle which had formerly been so peaceful, was now rife with robbery and violence, so that it was unsafe to travel.

For this same reason there was no question of our trying to return to our home and belongings. In any case, we had already heard that all communications had been severed and that most European houses had been looted and burned.

*　　*　　*

I could not imagine Jim leaving the jungle and his elephants for good; they had been part of him for so long.

In the main those men who had lived in the jungle, had divided themselves into three categories. There were those who had set about their work wholeheartedly and had become intent on absorbing all possible knowledge of everything about them. Then there were those who had light-heartedly flung the whole thing off with a couldn't-care-less attitude, looking on the life purely as a means of earning their living—they had taken things as they found them, and left nothing better for their contact. Lastly there were those who had been completely got down by the life, worrying about the loneliness and their health until they found themselves in the throes of a breakdown.

Jim had always been very much a member of the first category. Whatever he did he did wholeheartedly and to the best of his ability, but never taking himself too seriously and always retaining his sense of humour and fun.

Because fate had brought it about that his work had been

managing large herds of elephants, he made it his ambition to know all there was to know about them. Although unqualified, he was a capable vet, able to treat the animals in his care according to the most modern practices. At the same time he would never ignore the old native methods of the jungle Burman, who would sometimes travel miles through the jungle in search of a certain creeper which he knew would help to cure a sick animal.

Jim was always keen on efficient organisation and management, and the methods which he had introduced into Burma must have saved the timber companies thousands of pounds, for they were adopted everywhere throughout the country. In dealing with his elephants it was not only necessary to know all about the animals, but equally important to know all about the men who rode them. The oozie and his elephant have to work as one. The uncertain temper of an oozie riding a huge tusker could easily result in a valuable beast turning into a rogue killer.

The Burman is no less an enigma than all other orientals, and I believe Jim understood the way his mind worked as far as it is possible for any European to do. The selection and training of his oozies was given as much consideration as the management of the animals. In this he was wise, and his elephant men, shrewd in their judgment of man and beast, loved him and respected his foresight. When the war came he used all this knowledge, and was ready to rally his men and his elephants to the assistance of the hard-pressed Allied Forces.

General Sir William Slim, in a letter to Jim soon after the war, very generously wrote: "There were two of us Bills in the Fourteenth Army and I am not sure that 'Elephant' Bill was not the more famous of the two."

He was certainly known and respected throughout Burma for the great jungle man he was. His juniors loved him for his understanding and advice, for he was one of those rare human beings who can command through love as opposed to fear, persuade rather than drive. His superiors both in peace and in war respected him for the results he achieved, and the natural commonsense way in which he achieved them.

I found it difficult to believe that we should never return to the way of life we had lived for so long out here. But the country was now no longer the Burma we had known, and in a few months we sailed for England.

Chapter XXX

A LIFE TO THE FULL

WE docked at Southampton on a bleak morning at the end of February. The icicles were hanging from the roof of the customs shed, and I felt sorry for the four children as they stood huddled together on the quay while we went through the formalities. I had had warm clothes made for them before we left, but the long years in the East had made us forget how freezing an English winter could be.

Treve, usually so plucky, began to cry, Diana followed suit, and she turned to me, saying: "Why have we come to this horrid place? Can't we get back on the boat again now and go home?"

Apart from the general upheaval, they had all felt the parting with Naw Lah very acutely, as indeed I had myself. When we finally came away from India, Jim had arranged a special permit for her to return to her family in Lower Burma. The wrench with her had been sadder than all the other goodbyes that we had had to say, for she had shared our happy days as well as the sad ones, and had been with us for the whole of Treve's and Lamorna's lives. We never thought we would see her again, but as it so happened, later we did.

In the train on the way to Plymouth it was the greyness everywhere that struck the children most. Even during the cold weather in the East there had always been the brilliant sun shining from a permanently blue sky to light up the world around us.

We were on our way to Jim's mother's little house at St. Just in Cornwall. Although she and his father had both died, the house had been taken care of most beautifully in the meanwhile by Jeannette, his mother's Cornish housekeeper. For many years she had been a valued friend of the family, and still is to this day.

The welcome she had prepared for us warmed our hearts as well as our bodies. Even the baby Lamorna seemed to recognise that here was home, for as soon as she saw Jeannette she flung her arms round her neck and hugged her. Huge fires and a hot meal soon restored everyone's spirits, and in no time at all the children were dashing helter-skelter all over the house. They thought the lay-out extraordinary after the Eastern bungalows they were used to, and the grey granite of its walls at first seemed heavy and inhibiting. But like all children, after a day or two they seemed to have completely accepted their new surroundings.

Jim was full of joy at being back in his native Cornwall, and planned to settle down and enjoy his retirement here. But needless to say after only a few weeks he was longing to be doing some sort of work. One of the main occupations in this part of the country was bulb growing, so we decided we would try our hands at market gardening.

We bought hundredweights of daffodil bulbs and thousands of anemone corms, which we planted with meticulous care although everyone assured us we were in much too exposed a site to be successful. However, after a severe winter of blizzards and drifting snow, the following spring was a particularly mild one; our daffodils fetched fabulous prices, and the anemones came into bloom over and over again.

Flowers in those early years after the war were in great demand, as there were no regular supplies coming from abroad. We were handsomely rewarded for our care that first season and thought we were well on the way to making a fortune; but like so many others who have tried the same thing without enough experience, we soon found there were many snags.

215

The south-westerly gales swept across our land, searing every-thing in their path and nothing we could devise seemed enough to give protection from them.

In any case, I do not think that Jim was designed to be a market gardener—nor was he destined to be one for long. About this time he had a chance meeting with Sir Percy Lister, who offered him a job as managing director of a new firm which was about to introduce an insecticidal spraying machine into this country. Jim thought the project a good one, and accepted the position.

Normally it was to be an office job, but one of the first things he was called upon to do was to go to America to see the machine in operation. I stayed at home, still carrying on in a small way with the market garden; but prices had dropped to normal again now, and there was very little profit in it. However, the children were happily settled in school down here, and had grown to love the Cornish countryside, so we wanted to stay if possible.

Ever since we had got home the collection of stories Jim had written about his elephants while in hospital in Shillong, had been lying with a lot of other things in a drawer upstairs, almost forgotten. "You'd better keep it safely," he said. "You never know, we might make a hundred pounds out of it one day." When we had first arrived back, he had made one or two attempts to interest people in its publication, but nothing had come of it.

It so happened that while he was in America he was guest speaker at a business luncheon and had made references to his jungle life. Two reporters from the *New Yorker* magazine who were there asked him afterwards why he had not written a book. "I have," said Jim, "but nobody is the least interested in it."

Evidently these reporters were interested, for he told me that their hospitality had been quite overwhelming. After a series of visits to night clubs with them, he had walked down Fifth Avenue and was amazed to see his brother Tom coming along the street towards him. He had just started to say "What the devil are you doing in America?" when he realised he was talking to his own reflection in a mirror set at an angle on the pavement outside a jeweller's shop—he knew then that it was high time he went home to bed.

The whole incident was soon forgotten. But some months later, when he was back in England, he had a telephone call from Rupert Hart-Davis, the publisher. "I have been reading about you in an article in the *New Yorker* magazine," he said, "and it says amongst other things that you have written a book. I should like to see it."

No one was more surprised than Jim when about a week later he heard it was accepted for publication. "I don't suppose it is likely to sell much," he said.

About this time we had the sadness of parting with Diana and Michael, who had been part of our family for so long. Tom had married again, and he naturally wanted to have his children with him. Their going left a great blank and it was quite a year before Treve, now thirteen, could adjust himself, again, he missed them so much.

Jim was now in a well-paid job, but one so completely different from what he had been used to all his life that it did not surprise me when I saw that he was beginning to get restless. It was almost like imprisonment for him to be shut up in an office from morning to night after the complete freedom of the open-air life he had always enjoyed so close to nature in the forests and hills of Burma. It also meant that for the greater part of the time we were parted—he in London and we in Cornwall.

Deep down inside him Jim had always had the ambition to own land and to farm in Cornwall. He had often told me that during the unpleasant times of monsoons in Burma, memories of the sparkling sunlit Cornish sea and the clear lights and colours there, used to come to him like a far-off heaven, and made him determined that one day this ambition would be achieved.

The opportunity came in 1949. A farm came up for sale very close to where we were living, and we jumped at the chance. We both felt that it was more important to be together again and he working in congenial surroundings, than to have all the money in the world.

A few months later we were in the farm and faced with all its problems. It was tremendous hard work, but gave a life full of joy and interest to both of us, and to the children.

In May 1950 *Elephant Bill* was published. It made an immediate impact and from the beginning was a runaway success. Jim, being an extremely modest man, found this reception difficult to understand or believe. In a matter of months his name was a household word, and he was in great demand to lecture and make public appearances up and down the country.

He seemed quite as much at home, addressing an enormous audience packed into the Festival Hall in London, as he had been earlier on, doing the lonely job of teak extraction from the Burma jungle. He had quite a gift for lecturing and was able to relive his experiences in the jungle with his elephants, and recount them so vividly that one could almost see the animals walking across the platform in front of him.

He was most anxious that the farm should not suffer, but apart from all that was going on, he was blessed with an over-generous spirit. He was so proud and fond of the animals that he really felt great sorrow at parting with any one of them, and always managed to find some wonderful reason why an unprolific beast should be retained. Deep down I think he disliked the idea of any of the animals on his farm becoming victims of the butcher's knife.

I remember on one occasion he had a lovely bunch of South Devon steers looking at their best in the autumn—the time of the year when beef prices were also at their height. The local butcher visited the farm and made a very good offer for all seventeen animals. But Jim decided against selling, making the excuse that they would command a better figure if they were kept through the winter and sold in the spring. The cattle were tended very carefully all through the very hard winter months that followed. But when the spring came, the price quoted was much less than that offered before—they had, too, of course devoured a tremendous amount of winter keep in the meantime.

"What a pity we didn't accept the offer we had in the autumn," I said to Jim.

"Never mind, Sue," came the reply, "if we had sold them then we should have spent all the money by now."

I knew that he had really wanted those animals to live as long as he could possibly arrange it for them. He loved life so passionately himself that he wanted all in his care to enjoy their portion to the full. Such instincts do not contribute to profitable farming, and Jim's farm proved to be a steady drain on our financial resources. Nevertheless I knew it was something that he had to do, and while I shared with him the relief when after a few years it had to be sold, his life would have lacked something if he had not undertaken this venture.

It is wrong to count everything in terms of hard cash—as for the farm, who could assess the tremendous value we gained from it as a background for our children to grow up in and mature. These are priceless returns from life, never disclosed in any bank statement.

Before we left the farm, we had one great pleasure. A letter came from Naw Lah, telling us that the English family for whom she had been working in Calcutta were coming to England for six months. We wrote, asking her to spend her holiday, when it came, with us.

It was wonderful to see her again, and as always she adapted herself quite easily to the different background, even going so far as to bathe with Lamorna in the cold Cornish sea, and thoroughly enjoying it. She looked tiny beside Treve now, barely coming up to his shoulder.

When the family she was with eventually came back to live

in England for good, she came with them and is still in this
country. Whenever she gets the chance, she comes to stay
with us, and I hope always will. The children are now grown
up, but she still looks very much the same as she did when
she first arrived in Shwebo from her jungle village, all those
years ago.

In the meanwhile the book was going from strength to
strength as a record breaking best seller, and Jim felt encouraged
to begin on another, which he called *Bandoola*. The film
rights of both books were sold and he was asked to go to
Ceylon and then to Siam to find suitable locations for filming.
He took it all in his stride, but confessed to me that even now
he could not conceive himself being a well-known author.
He had, I think, been able to accept more easily the fame
that had come to him during the war, but to think of
himself as a writer of note only seemed to cause him great
amusement.

There was always this light touch about everything Jim
did. With most people as they mature, the colours of life tend
to fade and become less distinct; but for him they always
remained crisp and clear, sparkling and brilliant like the
colours of the Cornish sea on a bright June day. This basic
make-up shone continually through the many varied experiences of his life. He could get right down to fundamentals
as, gumbooted, he trod his farm, or feel equally at ease as
he dealt with his more sophisticated acquaintances in the
literary world. A pretty girl was always a pretty girl to Jim,
and he shared the enthusiasm of the young bloods in chasing
them. He had equal zest and happiness enjoying himself on
the crowded dance floor at the Café de Paris as he had in the
village, at home in the company of the local fishermen. But
it is not sufficient to describe him as a good mixer—he was
always so much more, and was able to become one of whatever company he was in.

I don't think he had any enemies. There were people
who disagreed with him and with whom he vehemently dis-

agreed, but when an argument became feverish he was usually the first to introduce reason and prevent things from going too far, and I can seldom recall ever having heard anyone describe him in other than affectionate terms.

We left the farm sadly—I say sadly because even though not successful with his farming, he still loved it. However, his life as an author was beginning to be a very busy one, involving a lot of travelling. It was an interesting time for both of us, as I was often able to go with him and we saw many new places and made many new friends.

Treve was now growing up, but the love of animals which he had always had was as strong as ever. He had decided to go to London University to study to be a vet; but in the meanwhile he had been abroad on National Service, and like his father in his early days, he also caught the wanderbug.

Australia appealed to him as a new country with great opportunities, and apart from the sadness of seeing him go we thought it an excellent thing, too. He sailed off when he was twenty, an independent figure determined to stand on his own feet without our help. He has been there now for four years making and paying his own way happily, and is working hard at his veterinary course.

Our final home together, Menwinnion, just above Lamorna Cove, did perhaps fulfill the dream that Jim had always had. For the first time in our lives there was a beautiful garden already made for us. Just beyond lay his favourite cliffs, where he would sit and write or paint; I don't think anyone could have been happier.

My last picture of him is in his old blue fisherman's jersey and corduroy trousers, mending a seat in one of the most sheltered corners of the garden. We were both sitting there chattering when Jeannette found us with a tray of tea. "I think I will use this corner to write in," was Jim's remark, but he never sat there again.

How sad was his going, and how ironic that after a life so full of hardships and dangers he should have died quite suddenly after an emergency appendicitis operation in Penzance Hospital.

*　　*　　*

While at work on this book and looking through Jim's papers I found in his desk these notes which he had written about himself, probably, I think, asked for by some American publisher about the time of his death in 1958. They are, perhaps, a better obituary than anyone else could have written about him.

BORN a Celt—my home in Cornwall—The Land's End, but to me the Land's beginning. The West of England my haven.

As a boy I was sometimes called a dreamer, but then my home spelt romance. My father had time to be my friend, and I never tired of his stories of travel and adventure prospecting in such romantic places as Australia, Brazil, South Africa, Spain and Portugal.

My mother was a lovely little Welsh woman who broke a very promising career at the Royal College of Music to marry. My two brothers and I were inseparable and as wild as March hares, for we had the unrestricted freedom of cliffs, caves, valleys and moors of a small peninsula.

Being without sisters I loved everyone else's with a deep passion—an important thing in life. I have at times experienced what many people would consider unbearable loneliness in jungles, deserts and cities with the utmost happiness and tranquillity. At other times I have taken the very essence of enjoyment out of any city where the opportunity has occurred. I have therefore seen both sides of life—and have enjoyed both to the full.

The loneliness and the life of the Burmese jungles was perhaps easier for me than others, for Cornwall being the background of my youth provided me with something that was fitting armour to see the world. It was neither money, pen, nor sword. It was a passionate understanding of nature, its kindness and its cruelty, love and sympathy. A realisation that powers of observation could make life easier. It was a complete trust in everything—nothing was a mystery.

It may seem strange perhaps to say I have so enjoyed solitude, but most people can, if they have some satisfying way of occupying their thoughts. My way has been from a very early age the companionship of animals. I have never studied them as a naturalist, but I have tried to establish an understanding with them, to find some common ground, some way of seeing the world through their eyes rather than through my own.

I never looked for a wren's nest, I merely walked to some spot where I thought one would build, stopped, then with sure hands parted the ferns, and in some mossy overhanging bank inserted two fingers into one of a dozen holes and felt ten warm eggs—mother wren might have shown it to me.

Long before I was of an age to carry a gun, I walked up snipe on a Cornish moor over Ruby my red setter. When she set a snipe, quivering with excitement, I would often say, "Yes, but you can't see it—I can." We shared the same thrill, she through her nose and I with my eyes, then we would flush it.

To count the waves on a bouldered foreshore during a south-west gale and know exactly which one would give up a piece of wreckage, just allowing time to grab it, was a suicide game if caught. I never was.

The instinct to create something in those youthful days was expressed in water colours—each one a masterpiece in my own eyes, yet each one hidden as a secret.

Such periods of sentimental dreaming alone were punctuated with dare-devil escapades in abandoned wrecks and old mine workings. With other boys life offered only adventure, we asked no questions as to any of the facts of life, everything explained itself.

As I grew up I squeezed the very essence out of life, with lots of laughter and some tears.

I am now back in Cornwall—my children living the same life as I did—those things do not change. I pray they too will go places and see things.